The New ALASKA COOKBOOK

2ND EDITION

The New ALASKA COOKBOOK

Recipes from the Last Frontier's Best Chefs

Kim Severson with Glenn Denkler

SASQUATCH BOOKS
SEATTLE

Printed in the United States of America
Distributed by PGW/Perseus
15 14 13 12 11 10 09   9 8 7 6 5 4 3 2 1

Cover design: Henry Quiroga
Interior design: Kate Basart
Second edition composition: Rosebud Eustace
Cover photographs: © Uppercutrf Royalty-Free / Inmagine
© Joe Klune / Dreamstime.com
Interior photographs:
© Monkey Business Images / Dreamstime.com
© Norman Pogson / Dreamstime.com
© John Wollwerth / Dreamstime.com
© Birgit Reitz-hofmann / Dreamstime.com
© Retina2020 / Dreamstime.com
© Bmaksym / Dreamstime.com

Project editor: Rachelle Longé
Indexer: Jean Mooney

Library of Congress Cataloging-in-Publication Data

Severson, Kim.
  The new Alaska cookbook : recipes from the last frontier's best chefs / Kim Severson with Glenn Denkler. -- 2nd ed.
      p. cm.
  Includes index.
  ISBN-13: 978-1-57061-604-4
  ISBN-10: 1-57061-604-3
  1. Cookery, American. 2. Cookery--Alaska. I. Denkler, Glenn. II. Title.
  TX715.S1462 2009
  641.59798--dc22
              2009009215

Sasquatch Books
119 S Main Street, Suite 400
Seattle, Washington 98104
(206) 467-4300
www.sasquatchbooks.com
custserv@sasquatchbooks.com

Contents

Recipe List

Acknowledgments

This second edition was made possible by several people: Glenn Denkler is at the top of that list. His drive and unending interest in food fueled this project. Thanks, too, to the chefs who happily donated their time and recipes. And a special tip of the hat to Gary and the rest of the team at Sasquatch Books, a publishing house that has always understood why cookbooks matter and why Alaska is special. Thanks also to my precious family for taking care of business while Mommy writes.

—*Kim Severson*

It has been a pleasure to be a conduit for the great chefs of Alaska. This second edition features four new chefs; thanks go to them for their passion for Alaskan food and their commitment to local sustainability. For the gift of the love of cooking brilliant food, I give thanks to my mom, Shirley. For a quick smile and unadulterated support, I thank my bride, Sheryl. For their discerning taste buds and good cheer, I thank the guinea pigs for all of the recipes tested: Vince Biciunas, Sue Blethen, David Carlsen, Margot Clemmens, Lee and Prentiss Cole, Jeni Cottrell, Warren Dillon, Travis Durnford, Shirley Erickson, Bill Grether, Ann and Rick Kaiser, Debby and Barry Meyers, Julia Milburn, Jane Palmer, Susann and Wolfgang Rossberg, Al Sutherland, Pam Went, and Sheryl. And a big thanks to my partner in crime for this book, still the best darned food writer in the whole wide world, Kim Severson.

—*Glenn Denkler*

Introduction

From my desk at *The New York Times*, I have a perfect view of the Port Authority parking lot and the traffic that piles up every day along Eighth Avenue.

Even though I know that anything I want to eat from just about anywhere in the world is only a few subway stops away, I often find myself homesick for what I found on my plate in Alaska.

I spent almost eight years as a journalist in Alaska, writing often about the state's home cooks and restaurant chefs. From there, I moved to San Francisco, drawn by a job writing about another kind of food and the promise of the bounty of Northern California. Then I landed here, where I still write about food in all its delicious political and social forms.

At every stop along the way, when people find out I lived in Alaska, they tease me about whale blubber. (Yes, there was whale blubber—in particular, a few potlucks featuring pink and black cubes of *maktak*, pronounced "muk-tuk," that had been dipped in seal oil.)

When an Alaskan who bragged about her ability to field-dress game was nominated for vice president in 2008, people wanted to know all about the best way to cook moose stew and whether a moose burger tasted like a beef hamburger. (The answer: Sort of.)

Chef Glenn Denkler, my co-author, and I both had the opportunity to return to Alaska recently. It had been almost a decade since we put together the first edition of this book. Since that time, the nation has intensified its love affair with farmers markets and organic food. The phrases "food miles" and "sustainable agriculture" have become household terms. Alaskan chefs are increasingly insisting on organic ingredients—although the practical cook using this book can of course substitute with non-organic items if budget or availability demands it. I would always, however, encourage the use of local food whenever possible. The taste is often superior, and you'll be helping a small-scale farmer or fisher or rancher survive.

Since the 1990s, the Internet and food blogging have made the world a much smaller place and built new kinds of communities around cooking. In Alaska, a place that is both an international crossroads and one of America's most isolated states, those kinds of global, digital connections—and a good system of air freight—can do wonders for a menu. Any serious eater who has visited Alaska leaves pleasantly surprised by the quality of the cuisine served in both city restaurants and remote fishing lodges. Chefs do especially wonderful things with the bounty from the state's rivers and oceans. They work with king crab legs close to 2 feet long, dense with batons of sweet meat, and ponder whether they would rather prepare the delicate cheeks of the halibut or a sturdy fillet—all just hours out of the water. Wild salmon, increasingly rare in the Lower 48, is so plentiful that chefs can experiment with different species and decide whether a fish from one river is fattier and more succulent than a fish from another.

I've heard chefs brag about the food from their particular region of the country, but I've never seen the sort of passion that pours forth when an Alaskan chef starts talking about the fat scallops of Kodiak Island or a cold, crisp oyster from Prince William Sound.

Alaska has other culinary gifts, too. Nearly round-the-clock daylight in the summer produces an abundance of herbs, greens, and other vegetables, including cabbages so big a single one might easily keep a restaurant in coleslaw for weeks. In the state's interior, morel mushrooms can grow as big as your fist. In the hands of skilled Alaskan chefs, such natural bounty becomes the sophisticated, regional food of the North.

The chefs who venture to Alaska are as resourceful—and sometimes as quirky—as many of the rest of the state's 650,000 residents. Like the prospectors of the Klondike Gold Rush, they moved north for adventure and opportunity and found it in kitchens from Juneau to Barrow. It's been that way since a band of European-trained chefs moved in just after Alaska achieved statehood in 1959. The 1980s saw an economic boom from oil and tourism, which sent Alaska's best chefs to hotels and cruise ships. In the 1990s, a renewed interest in regional food took hold, and Alaska's best chefs began opening their own restaurants and elevating the food served in remote lodges. Now, in the new century, Alaska continues to embrace its indigenous ingredients, and a new generation of more knowledgeable cooks and diners continues to make Alaska a more diverse and delicious place to eat.

In this revised edition, you'll still find some of the chefs who were in the previous one. Many of the people who were culinary leaders a decade ago remain so today, only now they have even more culinary experience under their toques and even better relationships with growers, fishers, and foragers. Others have moved on, with new talent taking their places.

You'll find both the old and the new in this book, which was the first to gather in one place the best recipes Alaska's best chefs have to offer. As it did when it was first issued, this cookbook reflects a style of Alaskan cooking that is strong on sophistication and light on Northern kitsch.

The recipes range from simple instructions for a perfect piece of alder-roasted salmon to more challenging fusion-influenced main dishes such as Sesame-Crusted Weathervane Scallops with Wild Mushrooms and Tomatillo Salsa. We've added dishes, like Ricotta Cavatelli with Alaskan Side-Striped Shrimp, that offer an easy method for making your own pasta, as well as simple weekday dishes like Soy Ginger King Salmon. You'll find elegant appetizers such as Ricotta Dungeness Crab Cakes and Vodka-Cured Gravlax and comforting desserts that include Warm Berry Crisp with Birch Syrup—and, of course, Baked Alaska.

Each recipe was tested by Glenn Denkler, a former hotshot restaurant chef from Anchorage who became one of the state's most respected culinary instructors. He can't stand a recipe that doesn't work, so you can trust that his translations of the chefs' recipes for the home cook are accurate.

Even in our second edition, only a handful of the state's chefs could be included. We apologize to those whom we left out; there are plenty of professionals across the state turning out food as good as the dishes contained in these pages. Nonetheless, we hope you find this book to be a workable, honest reflection of the cooking styles and personalities of the women and men who cook in the kitchens of the Last Frontier.

—*Kim Severson*

The Chefs

Jack Amon

Jack Amon claims he brought the sun-dried tomato to Alaska, and it may well be true. A self-taught, self-assured chef with Greek blood, Amon has led the Marx Bros. Cafe kitchen for more than twenty years. The little restaurant in an old house in downtown Anchorage boasts an 11,000-bottle wine cellar. It is the place many Alaskans go to celebrate new romances, new babies, and other life passages, including the coming of spring—an event worthy of a party in Alaska. The restaurant's reputation rests on Caesar salads made tableside, innovative use of products from Alaska's oceans and forests, and fusion-influenced dishes like macadamia nut–crusted halibut with Thai coconut curry. Amon grows a kitchen garden during the short, intense Alaska summer and takes his influence from the simple, straightforward approach of restaurants like Alice Waters's Chez Panisse in Berkeley, California.

Amon headed north in 1974 to work on the Trans-Alaska Pipeline. Although he had little kitchen experience, Amon ended up cooking in rough-neck camps and eventually talked his way into the best hotel kitchen in the state. In 1979, he opened the Marx Bros. Cafe with wine guru Van Hale and partner Ken Brown. Alaska had seen nothing like it. At the time, the notion of fine dining in Alaska was cherries jubilee and lobster tails. Amon recalls having to get up at 3 a.m. to order fresh arugula and strawberries from the Los Angeles produce markets. "Our goal was a restaurant that would rival any in the Pacific Northwest. We wanted to put Anchorage on the culinary map," he says. "Alaska has come a long way food-wise since then, but there's still plenty of room for innovation."

JoAnn Asher

JoAnn Asher believes that the best dining experiences are born from collaboration. That's why, on any given day, the menu at her stylish Sacks Cafe in downtown Anchorage will be built from several people's recipes—some of which she chose to include in this book. "You have to rely on other people to survive in Alaska. That's the approach we take in the kitchen," she says.

Asher, a world traveler and former waitress, drove from the San Francisco Bay Area to Alaska in an overstuffed Toyota in 1981. She met her former partner, Margie Brown, while they both worked at the Marx Bros. Cafe. At the time it was the hottest restaurant in Alaska. The pair decided to open Sacks in a little space downtown near the Anchorage Performing Arts Center in 1983. They began cooking a sort of upscale American regional food with Asian and Mediterranean twists and, of course, much of it centered on seafood. They eventually moved to a sleek, 84-seat space a few blocks away from their original location. "People say it looks like what you'd find in San Francisco or even New York. I say why can't we have this in Alaska?" Asher says. The menu continues to expand, including dishes as elevated as Asian five-spice scallops with carrot-ginger-coconut cream and as simple but creative as a sirloin burger with chipotle mayonnaise on a baguette. "Everyone calls our food New American," Asher says, "but it's really New Alaskan."

Michele Camera-Faurot

Reared by second-generation Italian parents in northeastern Pennsylvania, Michele Camera-Faurot has come a long way.

She recalls her grandmother scrutinizing a tomato just picked from the garden as if she were a jeweler inspecting a precious gem. As a result, Camera-Faurot absorbed her grandmother's talent for working with only the best ingredients and treating the bounty with passion and respect. Her great-uncle Freddie, a pharmacist in Brooklyn, would visit on the weekends with suitcases full of Italian cured meats and beautiful fresh cheeses, fruits, and sweets.

"To this day, their presence is strongly felt in my own kitchen, and I thank them every day," she says.

Equipped with a work permit, the 14-year-old began her restaurant career in a small local diner. At 17 she moved to New York City and briefly flirted with women's couture, selling retail on Madison Avenue. But fashion wasn't for her. A friend who owned a seafood market on the Upper West Side gave her a job behind the counter.

Under the tutelage of experienced fishmongers she soon moved up, learning to dress and handle seafood. Her first real cooking job was as an assistant to a very successful Chinese caterer, and Asian ingredients and techniques still influence her menus. Two years later, with the help of another cook, she was preparing 200 covers a night at the first outdoor café on New York's Upper West Side.

In the late 1990s she moved to Talkeetna, the staging town for Denali climbers, with her adventure-writer husband, and together they built Cafe

Michele. The restaurant opened in 2001 and was immediately ranked with the best places in Anchorage.

Today Michele and her son, Janus Leo, cook bistro-style fare using locally grown organic produce, free-range meats, and wild Alaskan seafood. Her restaurant is open from May through September. In the winter months, she is either busy with catering in Talkeetna or in Maui with her new catering adventure, Maui Palms.

Laura Cole

229 Parks is a restaurant of subtle sophistication that is a surprise to find in a remote area hours away from Alaska's two largest cities. The owner, Laura Cole, prepares dishes such as Pappardelle with Reindeer and Leeks in a beautiful restaurant about 8 miles from the south entrance of Denali National Park.

Originally from Detroit, Cole discovered Alaska through her husband, Land, whom she met in college in Olympia, Washington. His parents owned two lodges near Denali National Park, and her early experience washing dishes and assisting camp cooks made a strong impression.

She decided to attend culinary school, graduating from the New England Culinary Institute and then earning a master certificate for confections from the École de Gastronomie Française Ritz-Escoffier in Paris. With those credentials, she easily found a job at the well-regarded Marx Bros. Cafe in Anchorage. She then went back to her roots, taking over the kitchens at the two family lodges.

In 2005 she and her husband built 229 Parks, a nod to the restaurant's mile marker on the Parks Highway. The restaurant reflects the simple beauty of this wild, remote area. What makes the restaurant so special is Cole's commitment to the mission statement of the Chefs Collaborative, a national organization dedicated to sustainable food: "Promoting sustainable cuisine by teaching children, supporting local farmers, educating one another, and inspiring the public to choose good, clean food."

She has enlisted local growers utilizing sustainable practices to supply her with beautiful produce. Organic ingredients are de rigueur at 229 Parks, all the way down to organic sugar, meat, and dairy products. After the local growing season is over, she continues to use organic produce—ordered from Full Circle Farm in Washington—which is flown north through a special arrangement with Alaska Airlines.

Brett Custer

They call Brett Custer "Chef Shaggy." The *Scooby Doo* reference translates well in Homer, a fun, funky town of 5,000 whose nickname is the Cosmic Hamlet by the Sea. In Homer, which is literally at the end of the road on Alaska's Highway 1, halibut is the coin of the realm. That's fine with Custer. He's passionate about fresh seafood and local, organic produce.

Custer cooks at The Homestead Restaurant, a lovely log roadhouse filled with Alaskan art about 8 miles outside Homer. The restaurant opened in 1983 and is widely credited with bringing a new culinary sensibility to the little burg.

The menu reflects the bounty of Kachemak Bay and vegetables grown by local farmers. In the winter, the focus turns toward locals with two-for-one appetizers, lots of Alaskan oysters, and spice-rubbed prime rib carved from McNeil Canyon Meat Company roast.

Custer cooked his way through college in Greeley, Colorado. He was going to be a biologist but decided he wanted to see more of the country and cooking was a way to do that. He expanded his cooking skills under the watchful eyes of many chefs in the Lower 48, including Wolfgang Puck.

Like many chefs who end up in Alaska, Custer was simply following his heart. For nearly a dozen years he cooked around the state and in Homer before finding a perfect fit at The Homestead Restaurant, where the menu mixes local ingredients with Chef Shaggy's love of Asian and Mexican cuisine.

Kirsten Dixon

A decade ago, when we prepared the first edition of this book, we called Kirsten Dixon the "Martha Stewart of the North." And she still is. At the time she was arguably the best-known Alaskan cook, and her food still reflects both her sophistication and her relationship with the land surrounding her wilderness lodges. Dixon was the first to lead a group of Alaskan chefs to New York to cook at the prestigious James Beard House, and she has taken her comfortable Alaska-style cooking to Los Angeles, London, and more recently, to Australia, where she earned a master's degree in gastronomy from the University of Adelaide.

You'll need to take a plane to the lodges that make up her Within the Wild Alaskan adventure company: Winterlake Lodge, 198 trail miles northwest of Anchorage along Alaska's historic Iditarod Trail, and Redoubt Bay Lodge at Lake Clark Pass. The family sold the Riversong Lodge, which Dixon and her husband, Carl, left the medical profession to open in 1983. At press time they had acquired a third property, Tutka Bay Lodge, outside the seaside village of Homer along the Kachemak Bay.

They have now moved their headquarters to Winterlake. The consolidation has made the experience at the lodges even more special and has allowed the family more time to focus on giving guests a wilderness experience punctuated with excellent food and wine.

Dixon picked up many of her cooking skills from a parade of visiting chefs and foodies who teach classes at her lodges or work summers there.

The challenge of cooking in Alaska has always been the remoteness of her kitchens. Generators make walk-in temperatures uneven. Delicate foods need to be hand-carried and delivered by floatplane or ski plane. And although she travels as much as she can, Dixon often feels isolated from the larger food community. "Another challenge is the wildlife. We have bears that get into our kitchen, rip open the root cellar, break into freezers, and haul trash out of our dump area," she notes.

But the challenges are nothing when weighed against the life she has made with her husband and two daughters, who are now grown but still work in the food and hospitality business.

"I personally think we are doing some of the most unique food in Alaska," she says. "We make everything from scratch. Most of our foodstuffs are organic. We all take our kitchen very seriously."

Jens Hansen

Jens Hansen might well be called the father of new Alaskan cooking. At one time or another, many of Alaska's best chefs have spent time in his kitchen or as members of the Alaskan chefs' association he helped start. Hansen is a wild Dane with a deep passion for food and wine and something of a rogue's reputation in a state full of them.

Seeking adventure, Hansen came to Alaska in 1968 after formal training in Copenhagen and Paris. He got his feet wet in a hotel kitchen and then headed to the North Slope to cook for the people building the Alaska pipeline. But Hansen really hit his stride when he ran the Crow's Nest atop the Hotel Captain Cook in Anchorage during the wild, free-spending oil boom days in the late 1970s and early 1980s. During those years, Hansen and a handful of other classically trained Europeans like Hans Kruger had a profound impact on Alaska's professional kitchens. They demanded better produce from their purveyors and taught many old sourdoughs the delights of classic sauces and good wine. "When I came here there were only potatoes and cabbages. Really. There was not fresh meat. Nothing," he says. "Everybody thought I was nuts for my little tantrums over the lack of fresh vegetables or the quality of meat." In 1988, he opened his namesake restaurant, Jens' Restaurant, in a strip mall in the middle of Anchorage. Pepper steaks, perfect plates of sautéed fish, and traditional Danish dishes give way later in the evening to glasses of wine and singing in the bar. Every winter, he takes off for a month, flying to exotic locales like South Africa, New Zealand, and Belize. "You've got to travel, man," he says. "Otherwise it would be the same eight guys all copying each other."

Brett Knipmeyer

Brett Knipmeyer named his popular midtown Anchorage restaurant after his favorite person in the world: his daughter, Kinley.

The eclectic menu at Kinley's is a reflection of his time studying cooking in Portland, Oregon, and in the Chicago kitchens of Charlie Trotter. Halibut might be coated with cherry and apple cider beurre blanc and crusted with almonds; local rockfish is topped with shrimp salsa and basil emulsion; even a simple flank steak gets dressed up with Madeira and wild mushrooms.

As is the case with many chefs who settle in Alaska, Knipmeyer's trail to the Great Land was circuitous. Originally from Chicago, he left a career in architecture to follow his dream: he wanted to cook great food. He worked in kitchens in Colorado, Washington, and Oregon before receiving his culinary degree from Western Culinary Institute in Portland.

He returned to Chicago after culinary school to fine-tune his skills. Traveling around the world helped him broaden his life and his cooking experiences—after sampling smoked pig brains in a Hmong village in Thailand, he felt he "was open to about anything."

He had a 150-pound malamute named Sranger that offered new inspiration: why not explore the Alaskan mystique? He landed a job as chef at the much-loved Jens' Restaurant in Anchorage, where he stayed for seven years.

Feeling at home in Anchorage, he flexed his entrepreneurial muscle and opened Kinley's, a well-appointed but comfortable restaurant and bar that offers wine flights and wins particularly high marks from locals for service.

Farrokh Larijani

Farrokh Larijani grew up in Tehran, Iran, watching his father cook. When he was fourteen, his family moved to Seattle and he got his first restaurant job:

washing dishes in a steak house. He was hooked, eventually graduating from Portland's Western Culinary Institute. He was working for a chain of high-end restaurants in Seattle when the company offered to send him to one of two overseas properties. The choice: Alaska or Hawaii. "I took one look at my wife and she said, 'Let's give it a shot.'" It was the right call.

In 1996, two years after he arrived, Larijani was tapped to run the Glacier BrewHouse, Anchorage's sexy entry in the Northwest brewpub trend. With a wood-burning oven, an open-flame grill, and a rotisserie, Larijani built a strong menu featuring dishes like halibut with roasted corn salsa, thin-crusted pizzas with local wild mushrooms, and spit-roasted pork loin chops with garlic-infused mashed potatoes. His simple but sophisticated approach in the kitchen also helped define Orso, an Italian sister restaurant to the BrewHouse that opened next door in the summer of 2000. When he's not in one of the restaurants, you can find Larijani at a soccer game, raising scholarship money for culinary students, or mentoring a young cook.

Larijani says the best thing about cooking in Alaska is the wild fish, which is the envy of his chef friends in the Lower 48. But they don't envy how difficult it is to get good-quality seasonal produce, especially in the middle of a six-month-long winter. "You just have to bite the bullet sometimes" he says. "But that's the fun of it—dealing with the elements." Travel is the key for chefs in Alaska, he adds. "The bottom line is you've got to get out of the state to see what's hot and what's not."

David and JoAnn Lesh

Dave Lesh cooks in Gustavus, a tiny town clinging to the edge of Glacier Bay National Park in Southeast Alaska. The area was home for generations to Tlingit Indians, who built camps and smoked salmon there. White settlers and, later, back-to-nature hippies followed, helping to carve Gustavus's modern-day character. What's surprising is that for a town of four hundred in an isolated stretch of Alaskan wilderness, Gustavus has some extraordinary food. A hungry traveler might choose from pan-Asian and classic European dishes at the nearby Glacier Bay Country Inn or the homey, comforting food of the Gustavus Inn that Lesh and his wife, JoAnn, run.

Lesh's mother and father, Sally and Jack, homesteaded the site along the Salmon River almost 30 years ago. Sally was considered a fine cook, and her food drew travelers who had no other reason to head to Gustavus except to stay at the inn. Today, Lesh keeps the homespun tradition going but frequently adds new twists, whether it's a better sourdough pancake or a new method to prepare salmon. Dishes might include local morel mushrooms, fresh raspberries, and just-caught crab or sablefish. But no matter how tony food at the Gustavus Inn gets, visitors can always order Halibut Caddy Ganty, a rich mix of halibut, onions, sour cream, and mayonnaise that originated in Pelican, Alaska, and was made popular at the Gustavus Inn. The dish, often called Halibut Olympia, is now ubiquitous on menus all over the state. "What matters to people who eat here is that the food is honest and that it shows the best of what we've got growing around here," Lesh says.

Al Levinsohn

Al Levinsohn is now one of the grand masters of Alaskan food. Once the hot new chef in town, he has come into his own since he first landed in Alaska in 1984 to work at the Crow's Nest in the Hotel Captain Cook.

Levinsohn, author of *What's Cooking, Alaska?* (Sasquatch Books, 2008), has cooked everywhere from the Regal Hotel in Hong Kong to the James Beard House in New York City. He now runs his own restaurant in Anchorage called the Kincaid Grill, a sleek bistro where gumbo shares the menu with king crab cakes, Kodiak scallops, and perfectly roasted chops and steaks.

Getting to that point took a lot of work and some attitude adjustment, especially when he first moved north. Although the California-born chef had been coming to Alaska to visit since he was a child, he didn't realize the state's laid-back attitude would extend to one of the best kitchens in Anchorage at the time.

"I came from a strict background," he says. "I had to learn that Alaskans have a certain regimen that wasn't like any other professional kitchen I'd been in."

It didn't take him long to settle in. After that first job he went on to run the kitchens in the Regal Alaskan Hotel. He was only 23. Next, he opened the well-appointed Alyeska Prince Hotel in the ski resort 40 miles south of Anchorage.

After a short stint as the opening chef for the Glacier BrewHouse, he returned to the Alyeska Resort as executive chef of the finest hotel property in the state. There he watched over five restaurants, including a traditional teppanyaki grill and the innovative Seven Glaciers at the top of Mount Alyeska, accessible only by a 60-passenger tram.

Through it all, the challenges of cooking in Alaska have changed, he notes. For one thing, much better produce is available. "It was rough in the early 1980s—you'd get cases of yellowed, flowered broccoli and that was it. Take it or leave it."

Now availability is better and so is the state's collective palate. That is both good and bad. "Used to be you could blow people away pretty easily with new and different stuff they'd never seen," he says. "Now it takes more work to really wow people."

Jens Nannestad

Jens Nannestad's food is upscale but accessible, innovative but not over the top. The combination makes his Anchorage restaurant, Southside Bistro, one of the gems of Alaskan dining. "We have quite a sophisticated clientele up here, but we have to realize we're in Alaska and not get too 'Aqua' on them," he says, referring to the four-star San Francisco restaurant. It's no surprise that Nannestad would reference the Bay Area restaurant scene—for a decade he traveled between Alaska and Northern California before putting down roots up north in the mid-1990s. He started his career in Austria, as an apprentice for a demanding chef, and later graduated from the California Culinary Academy.

Nannestad landed in Alaska in 1985 and worked in the Hotel Captain Cook's top restaurant, the Crow's Nest. The young immigrant got his green card and headed back to the Bay Area. He took a job as a chef on a cruise ship and met his wife and business partner, Megan. They settled in Alaska. After a couple of jobs in other people's kitchens, Nannestad opened Southside Bistro in 1995. His biggest challenge remains finding talent, particularly cooks with a formal culinary education. He feels lucky to have found his chef de cuisine, Alaska-born Elizabeth King, and even includes some of her recipes in this book. Like most professional chefs in Alaska, Nannestad has no plans to leave: "There's still some fun left in it here. It's not so competitive, so it's still entertaining."

A Note about the Recipes

from Chef Glenn Denkler

Recipes are interesting phenomena. By themselves, many recipes have probably intimidated or turned off oodles of potential cooks. What a shame! Let me attempt to demystify the process.

The culinary profession is divided into two groups of folks: bakers and cooks. Cooks use recipes as a guideline in preparing food. Professional bakers don't call recipes "recipes"; they call them formulas. The ingredients in formulas react with each other in an exact scientific way, so measurements must be precise. On the other hand, cooks focus more on a recipe as a general guideline that they can be flexible with.

The point is that in cooking, flavors are not static. Two tomatoes from the same bin may have different tastes. Fresh basil purchased from one store may be more intense than a bunch from another. A recipe should be considered a starting point. A cook must learn to taste and not be a slave to a recipe. Food must be continually tasted and flavors adjusted during the cooking process. The more a cook tastes, the better the cook.

So, treat these recipes with respect; respect the talent of the cooks who came up with the ideas, but have fun. If you don't like an ingredient or amount, be bold and experiment. If you can't get wild Alaskan salmon or Kodiak scallops, find the best seafood you can, given the state of your local fish market. Cultivated mushrooms can substitute for wild ones in a pinch. Asparagus can work in place of fiddleheads, and so on. (Of course, be more careful with the desserts.) Let your heart and your taste buds rule.

A Couple of Technical Points and Tips

- Temperatures are offered in Fahrenheit.
- Eggs are large.
- Buy the best products you can afford; local, if possible. You will be rewarded.
- Read the recipe completely through; gather all the ingredients, cooking pans, and utensils; and preheat the oven if necessary before beginning to cook.

Appetizers

Alaskan Smoked Salmon Bruschetta

Al Levinsohn, Kincaid Grill

Smoked salmon is everywhere in Alaska. Many people have home smokers or bring their summer's catch to professional meat and fish processors for smoking or for lox. This dish is a quick starter that can be thrown together if friends drop by. Other smoked fish may be substituted.

½ cup diced (¼ inch) ripe tomatoes
¼ cup thinly sliced fresh basil
2 tablespoons feta
¼ cup flaked smoked Alaskan king salmon
12 slices baguette, cut on the bias ½ inch thick
¼ cup extra-virgin olive oil

✤ Preheat the oven to 400°F.

✤ Combine the tomatoes, basil, feta, and salmon in a small bowl. Set aside.

✤ Brush each slice of bread on both sides with olive oil. Place the slices of bread on a cookie sheet and toast in the oven until well browned and crisp. Remove from the oven and allow bread to cool to room temperature.

✤ Top each slice of toast with an equal amount of the salmon mixture.

SERVES FOUR

Pan-Seared Alaskan Oysters with Fennel and Leeks

Kirsten Dixon, Within the Wild Lodges

Because the water in Alaska is so cold, oysters don't reproduce. That makes for crisp, firm oysters year-round. The trade-off, however, is that the handful of professional oyster growers have to import Pacific oyster spat from Washington.

This oyster appetizer has become a popular first course at Within the Wild Lodges. Dixon serves it in some variation all year long. She adds trimmed pieces of fennel to the reducing cream for flavor. Sometimes she deep-fries the oysters with a panko (Japanese bread crumb) crust. She likes to use deep-fried basil as a garnish, as well.

24 fresh Alaskan oysters
2 cups heavy cream
1 medium fennel bulb, trimmed and quartered
1 tablespoon butter
2 small leeks, trimmed and halved
2 tablespoons grapeseed oil
24 white pearl onions, peeled and blanched
Ground sea salt and ground white pepper

⚜ Shuck the oysters, reserving their liquor. Strain the liquor through rinsed cheese-cloth and pour into a medium saucepan. Add the cream. Bring the cream and liquor mixture just to a simmer, then reduce the heat to low, and reduce the sauce slowly by half.

⚜ In a medium sauté pan over medium heat, fry the fennel in butter until tender. Reduce the heat to low and add the leeks. Cover and cook until soft. Remove fennel and leeks and keep warm.

⚜ Refresh the onions in a saucepan of simmering water for 1 minute.

⚜ Add the grapeseed oil to the sauté pan and increase the heat to medium-high. Pan-sear oysters for about 1 minute on each side.

⚜ Pour about ¼ cup of the reduced cream and oyster liquor sauce onto warmed plates. Place 6 oysters on each plate. Add leek, 1 fennel quarter, and 6 pearl onions. Season with salt and pepper to taste.

SERVES FOUR

Alaskan Oysters on the Half Shell with Pineapple-Sake Mignonette

Brett Knipmeyer, Kinley's Restaurant & Bar

Instead of the typical splash of hot sauce, Knipmeyer treats these gems with a bit more subtlety. If no sake is on hand, a white wine would do just fine.

2 dozen fresh oysters
3 cups baby mixed lettuces

PINEAPPLE-SAKE MIGNONETTE

½ pineapple, peeled, cored, and puréed
Sake
3 medium serrano peppers, thinly sliced
¼ teaspoon freshly cracked black pepper
1 tablespoon minced shallot
Salt

⚜ To make the oysters, shuck and discard top shell. Divide the lettuces among 4 plates. Place 6 oysters on each plate.

⚜ To make the mignonette, first measure the amount of pineapple purée. Then measure an equal amount of sake. Combine the pineapple purée, sake, serrano peppers, pepper, and shallot, mixing well. Season with salt.

⚜ Top each oyster with a generous portion of mignonette.

SERVES FOUR

Curried Halibut Egg Rolls with Sweet Chili–Mango Sauce

Brett Custer, The Homestead Restaurant

Wondering what to do with the leftover halibut from last night's dinner or that fillet sitting in the freezer? Turn it into a sublime love fest with these egg rolls. Any mixture of vegetables that you come up with as an accompaniment would work well, but the mango sauce is sublime.

SWEET CHILI–MANGO SAUCE

1 cup diced fresh mango

½ cup Mae Ploy sweet chili sauce

1 teaspoon minced garlic

1 teaspoon minced fresh ginger

2 tablespoons chopped cilantro

½ teaspoon Thai fish sauce (available in Asian markets)

ASIAN VEGETABLES

2 tablespoons sesame oil

½ cup julienned carrots

½ cup julienned red peppers

1 cup sliced oyster mushrooms

1 cup roughly chopped napa cabbage

2 tablespoons soy sauce

½ teaspoon minced garlic

½ teaspoon minced fresh ginger

CURRIED HALIBUT EGG ROLLS

2 tablespoons curry paste (yellow or red)

One 13-ounce can coconut milk

1 pound cooked halibut, cooled

8 egg roll wrappers (available in Asian markets)

1 egg white, beaten

⅓ cup rice flour

Peanut oil for frying

✢ To make the mango sauce, blend all ingredients in a blender or food processor until smooth. Reserve.

✢ To make the Asian vegetables, heat the sesame oil in a deep pan over high heat until it shimmers. Add carrots, red peppers, and mushrooms and stir-fry for 2 minutes. Add cabbage and soy sauce, stir, and cover for 1 minute. Remove lid, stir in garlic and ginger. Cook, stirring, for 15 seconds; remove from heat and allow vegetables to cool.

✢ To make the egg rolls, in a large bowl mix curry paste and coconut milk. Break up halibut into chunks and add to curry mixture. Lay out an egg roll wrapper like a diamond. Place an eighth of the halibut mixture and an eighth of the Asian vegetable mixture near the bottom of the wrapper. Roll the bottom of the wrapper just over the filling and then tuck in sides and finish rolling. Seal with egg white and roll in rice flour. Repeat seven times. Add enough peanut oil in a deep pan to cover egg rolls; heat over medium-high heat until oil registers 350°F on a deep-fat thermometer. Fry egg rolls until crispy, 3 to 5 minutes; drain on paper towels. Serve with mango sauce on the side.

SERVES FOUR

Pistachio-Crusted Pâté de Campagne

Brett Knipmeyer and Jim Nyholm, Kinley's Restaurant & Bar

*Knipmeyer and Nyholm debunk the mystery behind great country-style pâté with this rec-
ipe. Just remember the importance of keeping the forcemeat well chilled during the process.
This ensures not only the perfect texture of a good pâté, but also guarantees a safe product.
Chicken liver may be substituted for the duck liver.*

PÂTÉ DE CAMPAGNE

1½ pounds boneless pork butt, cubed

8 ounces duck liver

3 eggs

2 tablespoons minced shallot

1 tablespoon Quatre Épices (recipe follows)

1½ teaspoons salt

½ teaspoon freshly ground black pepper

¼ cup cognac

Bacon slices to cover

⅓ cup toasted chopped pistachios

GARNISHES

½ cup orange marmalade

¼ cup dried currants

2 tablespoons red wine

1 cup Dijon mustard

1 tablespoon chopped fresh tarragon

1 cup capers

1 cup cornichons

2 cups baby lettuce

4 thin slices red onion

Toast points

✦ To make the pâté, preheat the oven to 275°F. Pulse the pork butt in a food processor until ground. Refrigerate. Process duck liver, eggs, shallot, quatre épices,
salt, pepper, and cognac until smooth. Force the mixture through a strainer with
the back of a spoon to ensure smoothness. Put the liver mixture in a bowl that
is resting in a larger bowl half filled with ice. Add the ground pork to the liver
mixture. Fry a small amount of mixture in a sauté pan. Taste and adjust seasoning.

Line the inside of a small loaf pan or terrine completely with plastic wrap. Fill the pan with pâté to just below the top. Place strips of bacon on top to cover. In the preheated oven, cook in a water bath until internal temperature in the center of pâté registers 150°F when measured with an instant-read thermometer, about 1½ hours. Place a light weight on top of the bacon; refrigerate pâté overnight. Remove bacon and gently ease pâté out of pan. Unwrap and press pistachios into pâté. Slice the pâté into 8 slices.

✦ To make the garnishes, mix together the marmalade, currants, and red wine; divide among 4 small bowls. Mix the mustard and tarragon; divide among 4 small bowls. Divide the capers among 4 small bowls. Divide the cornichons among 4 small bowls.

✦ To serve, divide the lettuce among 4 chilled plates, top with red onion slices, and place 2 pâté slices on each plate. Serve with toast points and bowls of the garnishes.

SERVES FOUR

Quatre Épices

4 teaspoons black peppercorns
1 teaspoon whole cloves
2 teaspoons freshly grated nutmeg
1 teaspoon ground ginger

✦ Grind the peppercorns and cloves in a spice grinder. Combine pepper-clove mixture with nutmeg and ginger. Seal tightly and store at room temperature for up to 5 months.

MAKES 8 TEASPOONS

Deviled Crab Cakes with Red Chile Mayonnaise

Jack Amon, The Marx Bros. Cafe

Crab is plentiful during the fall and winter. Alaskans eat compact, meaty Dungeness from Southeast and impossibly big king crab from the Bering Sea off the western edge of the state. These crab cakes have long been a favorite at the Marx Bros. Cafe. The mayonnaise is just spicy enough to give the crab cakes a kick without overpowering them.

1 tablespoon butter

2 teaspoons minced onion

¼ teaspoon minced garlic

1 tablespoon minced red pepper

1 tablespoon minced yellow pepper

4 teaspoons flour

⅓ cup heavy cream

1 teaspoon dry mustard

2 teaspoons prepared mustard

2 teaspoons mixed herbs, such as basil, parsley, and/or chives

¼ teaspoon cayenne

Dash of Tabasco

1 egg yolk

10 ounces Dungeness crabmeat, picked over, rinsed if salted

1 teaspoon fresh lemon juice

1¼ cups fresh bread crumbs

1 cup milk

1 egg

Clarified Butter, for frying (page 203)

Romaine lettuce, thinly sliced

Red Chile Mayonnaise (recipe follows)

✤ Melt the butter in a skillet. Add the onion, garlic, and peppers. Cook over low heat 2 to 3 minutes. Add the flour and stir until well incorporated. Cook 2 to 3 minutes more, but do not allow it to brown. Gradually add the cream and stir until thickened. Add the dry and prepared mustards, herbs, cayenne, and Tabasco, mixing well. Stir in the egg yolk. Quickly add the crabmeat, lemon juice, and ¼ cup of the bread crumbs, stirring until well blended. Remove from the heat and refrigerate for 4 hours or overnight.

✢ Divide the chilled mixture into 12 equal portions. Shape each one carefully into an oval. Whip the milk and egg together. Dip the crab ovals into the egg-milk mixture, then into the remaining 1 cup bread crumbs.

✢ Fry the crab ovals in clarified butter until golden brown on each side. Drain on paper towels. Serve three per person on a bed of thinly sliced Romaine lettuce with a dollop of red chile mayonnaise.

SERVES FOUR

Red Chile Mayonnaise

1 teaspoon *sambal oelek* (Thai chile sauce, available at Asian markets)
3 cloves garlic
4 tablespoons fresh lime juice
2 tablespoons prepared mustard
2 eggs
1 cup olive oil
1 cup vegetable oil
Salt and freshly ground black pepper

✢ Combine the *sambal oelek* with the garlic and lime juice in a food processor. Add the mustard and eggs. Process until well mixed. With the processor running, add a fourth of the oil, 1 tablespoon at a time. With the processor still running, add the remainder of the oil in a thin, steady stream. Adjust the seasoning with salt and pepper to taste.

MAKES 2½ CUPS

Spot Prawn Bows with Saffron Aïoli

Laura Cole, 229 Parks Restaurant and Tavern

Spot prawns have been the rage in Alaska and Canada for years. A cold-water crustacean, spot prawns are sweet and more tender than their warm-water cousins. They are caught in pots, a method that is environmentally very sound as there is virtually no bycatch or habitat damage. Unfortunately, they have been overfished in most areas of Alaska and are recently available only in southeast Alaska and British Columbia. Feel free to substitute local fresh shrimp.

SAFFRON AÏOLI

>   1 tablespoon white wine
>   2 tablespoons water
>   Generous pinch of saffron threads
>   3 large cloves garlic
>   ½ teaspoon sea salt (Maldon preferred)
>   2 free-range egg yolks
>   ¾ cup organic extra-virgin olive oil

PRAWNS

>   Organic vegetable oil for frying
>   8 organic basil leaves
>   Eight 4-inch squares phyllo pastry
>   8 spot prawns (26–30 per pound), peeled
>   Sea salt and freshly ground black pepper

✣ To make the saffron aïoli, simmer the white wine, water, and saffron in a small saucepan until the mixture reaches syrup consistency; be careful not to burn. In a food processor, mix the saffron syrup, garlic, salt, egg yolks, and 1 tablespoon of the olive oil for 30 seconds, scrape down the bowl, then process for another 30 seconds. Scrape down the bowl again. With the processor running, add the remaining oil in a slow, steady drizzle until it is all incorporated. (If you add the oil too quickly, the aïoli will not emulsify properly.) The aïoli may be refrigerated for 4 days.

⚜ To make the prawns, add enough oil in a deep pan to cover prawn bows; heat over medium-high heat until oil registers 375°F on a deep-fat thermometer. Place a basil leaf at a corner of each square of phyllo, top with a prawn, and season with salt and pepper. Wrap basil/prawn tightly in phyllo, twisting the ends of the phyllo in opposite directions to form a bow. Fry prawn bows in batches until pastry is crispy and slightly browned, about 45 seconds to 1 minute. Drain on paper towels. Serve with a side of saffron aïoli.

SERVES FOUR AS AN APPETIZER

Forest Mushroom Tarts

Kirsten Dixon, Within the Wild Lodges

Eating from the land matters to many Alaskans, even if it is a just few wild berries or one of the easily identifiable edible mushrooms that grow in many parts of the state. Morels pop up in the spring and King boletes, or porcinis, grow all summer and into early fall.

For these tarts, blanch the mushrooms so that they don't release moisture and make the crusts soggy.

½ cup heavy cream
1 tablespoon plus 1 teaspoon plus 2 teaspoons butter
1 large leek, cleaned, trimmed, and sliced
Salt and freshly ground black pepper
1 pound porcini or other wild mushrooms, stems removed and discarded
Four 5-inch-square sheets of puff pastry
4 teaspoons fresh thyme
1 clove garlic, minced
2 tablespoons grapeseed oil

✦ Preheat the oven to 400°F.

✦ In a medium pot, bring to a boil enough water to cover the mushrooms.

✦ At the same time, pour the cream into a saucepan and bring to a very gentle simmer.

✦ Melt 1 tablespoon of butter in a medium sauté pan over medium heat and add the leek. Reduce the heat to low, cover, and cook just until soft, 6 to 8 minutes. Add the leeks to the cream and simmer over medium heat until the cream reduces by half and glazes the leeks. Season with salt and pepper to taste.

✦ Cook the mushrooms in the boiling water for 3 minutes, drain, and rinse. Heat a small sauté pan over medium heat. Add 1 teaspoon of butter. Add the mushrooms and cook until all the moisture is evaporated. Set aside.

✦ Lay out the puff pastry sheets on a floured work surface, and sprinkle with thyme and pepper. Use a rolling pin to press the thyme and pepper into the dough and to stretch out the sheets by ½ inch. Cut each sheet into a 4-inch circle. Prick the pastry all over with the tines of a fork. Place the sheets on a jelly-roll pan lined with parchment paper. Brush the tops of the circles with the remaining 2 teaspoons butter.

✣ Spread a fourth of the leek-cream mixture on each circle, leaving a 1-inch border. Layer the mushrooms on top of the leeks. Combine the garlic and grapeseed oil. Brush half of this mixture over the tarts.

✣ Bake the tarts until golden brown, checking after 10 minutes. Remove from the oven and brush with remaining garlic-oil mixture. Serve right away.

SERVES FOUR

Into the Forest

On the way home from a three-day hike through Denali National Park, we stopped to stretch our legs. There, just a few yards from the car, was the largest hedgehog mushroom I had ever seen. We walked a little deeper into the woods and patches of the tan mushrooms blanketed the forest floor. We dropped to our knees and gathered as many as we could carry home. The next night, I made a big pot of hedgehog soup with plenty of cream and sherry.

Foraging for mushrooms and other forest edibles is common practice all over Alaska. In the interior, forest fires mark the land and make prime territory for spring's elusive morel mushroom. In the fall, king boletes, called cèpes in France and porcini in Italy, grow readily. A few days foraging in the fall and a good supply can be dried for winter.

But mushrooms aren't the only gems in Alaska's forest. In the southeast, the tips of young spruce are gathered to make beer and jam. Young, tightly coiled ostrich fern fronds are a wonderful spring treat. Called fiddleheads, they resemble the curved end of a violin. When the shoots have just pushed their way through the earth, they are perfect for sautéing in nothing but butter and a sprinkle of salt. They taste grassy and green, like asparagus.

Berries of all sorts are the food of high summer, and have long played an important part in the diets of Alaska Natives. Black and red currants, raspberries, cranberries, blackberries, and a host of other berries grow throughout Alaska. Blueberries are a particular pleasure, and they end up in a year-round parade of jams, jellies, and pancakes. The careful cook makes sure several containers are put in the freezer, preserving the abundance of summer to use during the long winter.

Fireweed makes for sweet honey, and rose hips can be dried and boiled into tea or made into jam. Even snow sweetened with a little birch syrup can be a delightful way to enjoy a taste of Alaskan wilderness in the middle of winter.

—Kim Severson

Oysters in Saffron Cream with Caviar

Jack Amon, The Marx Bros. Cafe

Alaskan oysters are grown in stacked nets called lantern nets that hang in the icy water. Because the oysters aren't fighting the tides or predators on the beach, they can put energy into growing meat rather than shell. The result is an oyster with a deep cup full of steely, crisp meat. Pour a flute of Champagne and serve these rich, beautiful oysters for a special occasion. Caviar gives the oysters an extra-elegant touch. If money is tight, they can be served without the caviar, but they are so much nicer with it.

24 large oysters
1½ cups dry Champagne or sparkling wine
Pinch of saffron threads
1½ cups heavy cream
6 tablespoons butter, cut into 1-tablespoon pieces
Salt and ground white pepper
2 ounces sevruga caviar

✦ Preheat the oven to 250°F.

✦ Shuck the oysters and leave in the 24 cups. Place the 24 shell bottoms on a pan lined with parchment paper and place in the oven.

✦ Bring the Champagne to a boil in a small saucepan. Add the saffron and reduce by a third.

✦ Add the cream and reduce until quite thick. Turn off the heat and add the oysters. Shake in the pan and let stand for 2 to 3 minutes.

✦ Place the oysters in the heated shells. Return the sauce to the heat. Reduce until thick. Remove from the heat. Whisk in the butter, piece by piece. When all butter is incorporated, taste for seasoning and add salt and pepper to taste.

✦ Divide the oysters among 6 plates. Spoon the sauce over the oysters. Top each with an equal amount of caviar. Serve right away.

SERVES SIX

Island Sweet Chili Shrimp Cocktail

Michele Camera-Faurot, Cafe Michele

Camera-Faurot has spent part of each winter for the past 16 years in Hawaii. Her love of the islands and their natural ingredients are the inspirations for this recipe.

2 pounds large shrimp (13–15 or 16–20 per pound)
4 quarts Court Bouillon (page 193)
⅓ cup sesame oil
¼ cup Mae Ploy sweet chili sauce
¾ cup chopped fresh pineapple
1 cup 1-inch square-cut bell peppers (red, yellow, and orange)
½ cup sliced green onion
¼ cup minced red onion
1½ teaspoons minced garlic
1 tablespoon minced fresh ginger
¼ cup chopped cilantro
2 tablespoons chopped mint
Juice of 4 limes
4 cups thinly shredded red cabbage

✤ Poach the shrimp in the court bouillon (the liquid should be steaming) until shrimp are just cooked through, about 8 minutes for size 13–15 shrimp or 6 minutes for size 16–20. Peel and devein the shrimp. In a large bowl, toss the shrimp in the sesame oil, cover, and refrigerate for a minimum of 2 hours. Add the chili sauce, pineapple, bell peppers, green onion, red onion, garlic, ginger, cilantro, and mint. Refrigerate for another 2 hours. Add lime juice and mix well.

✤ To serve, fill 6 large margarita glasses with the shrimp mixture. Place the glasses on small plates and surround the base of the glasses with red cabbage.

SERVES SIX

King Salmon "Pâté"

Michele Camera-Faurot, Cafe Michele

A favorite at Cafe Michele, this is more like a spread than a classic pâté. The rich salmon is bound with a fresh caper mayonnaise, making it a crowd-pleaser. Camera-Faurot serves it with focaccia bread sticks that are toasted and then brushed with garlic oil.

CAPER MAYONNAISE

    2 organic egg yolks

    3 tablespoons capers

    2 tablespoons fresh lemon juice

    2 tablespoons lemon zest

    1 tablespoon Dijon mustard

    2 cups light or regular olive oil (not extra-virgin)

    Salt

SALMON

    2 cups white wine

    1½-pound skinless king salmon fillet

    ½ cup finely diced red onion

    ½ cup finely sliced green onion (white and green parts)

    ½ cup finely diced celery

    3 tablespoons chopped fresh dill

    1½ cups caper mayonnaise

    Salt and freshly ground black pepper

⚜ To make the caper mayonnaise, place the egg yolks, capers, lemon juice, lemon zest, mustard, and one tablespoon of the olive oil in a food processor. Process for 1 minute. With the processor running, add the remaining olive oil in a slow, thin stream. Season with salt. Refrigerate for up to 4 days.

⚜ To make the salmon, in a large sauté pan bring 2 cups water and white wine to a simmer. Reduce temperature until the liquid is at the poaching point (steaming). Add the salmon and poach until the fish is just done (about 8 minutes, depending on thickness), then remove from liquid and place in a large bowl. Shred the salmon with a fork. Allow it to cool at room temperature for 20 minutes, then cover and refrigerate for at least 3 hours. When the salmon is chilled, fold in red onion, green onion, celery, dill, and caper mayonnaise. Season with salt and pepper. Chill before serving.

SERVES SIX

Alaskan King Crab Cakes with Dijon-Dill Aïoli

Brett Custer, The Homestead Restaurant

Perhaps one of the most common uses for this delightful crustacean is the crab cake. Custer moves it up a notch with his take on a traditional favorite. Feel free to substitute any fresh herb or a combination of herbs in the aïoli.

DIJON-DILL AÏOLI

    2 egg yolks
    3 cloves garlic, chopped
    1 teaspoon fresh lemon juice
    ¼ cup Dijon mustard
    1 tablespoon chopped fresh dill
    1 cup olive oil
    Salt and freshly ground black pepper

ALASKAN KING CRAB CAKES

    ½ cup finely diced red pepper
    ½ cup finely diced yellow onion
    ½ cup very finely diced carrot
    2 tablespoons butter
    1 tablespoon minced garlic
    1 pound king crabmeat
    1 cup cooked and mashed potatoes
    ½ cup Dijon mustard
    1 teaspoon ground chipotle pepper
    1 cup panko (Japanese bread crumbs, available in Asian markets and some supermarkets)
    2 eggs
    Panko for coating
    ½ cup Clarified Butter (page 203)

⚜ To make the aïoli, in a food processor process egg yolks, garlic, lemon juice, mustard, and dill with 1 tablespoon of the olive oil for 30 seconds. With the processor running, add the remaining oil in a slow drizzle. Season with salt and pepper; reserve. May be refrigerated for 4 days for later use.

⚜ To make the crab cakes, sauté red pepper, onion, and carrot in butter until onions are translucent, about 4 to 5 minutes. Add garlic, cook for 10 seconds;

allow mixture to cool. In a large bowl, break crab into small to medium chunks. Add cooled vegetables, potatoes, mustard, chipotle, and panko; mix well. Add eggs; mix well. Divide mixture into 8 portions, flatten, and press both sides into panko. Place cakes on a parchment-paper-lined pan and freeze for 30 minutes. Pan-fry the crab cakes in clarified butter until golden on each side and no more than 2 minutes total. Drain on paper towels.

✦ To serve, divide the crab cakes among 4 warm plates. Drizzle with aïoli.

SERVES EIGHT AS AN APPETIZER OR FOUR AS AN ENTRÉE

Salmon Croquettes with Jalapeño Aïoli

Farrokh Larijani, Glacier BrewHouse

Most Alaskan cooks will tell you their summer menus always have room for good ways to use leftover salmon. This is a comforting, homey dish that puts all that extra fish to good use.

SALMON MIXTURE

1½ cups fresh salmon, cooked and flaked

2 tablespoons finely diced onion

½ cup (packed) grated pepper Jack cheese

2 tablespoons mayonnaise

2 teaspoons minced jalapeño, seeded if you like

1½ teaspoons minced chipotle chile

1 tablespoon chopped cilantro

½ teaspoon kosher salt

1 tablespoon minced red pepper

1 egg white, lightly beaten

2 tablespoons panko (Japanese bread crumbs, available in Asian markets and some supermarkets)

BREADING

Peanut or vegetable oil

1 cup panko

1 cup cornmeal

4 egg whites, lightly beaten

GARNISH

12 avocado slices

1 cup Marinated Cabbage (recipe follows)

4 tablespoons Jalapeño Aïoli (recipe follows)

4 lemon wedges

8 sprigs of cilantro

✦ Gently mix together the salmon, onion, cheese, mayonnaise, jalapeño, chipotle, cilantro, salt, and red pepper until well combined. Add the egg white and 2 tablespoons panko and combine. Shape into 4 patties. Refrigerate for at least 1 hour.

✤ Heat the oil to 350°F in a pan deep enough so the oil comes halfway up the sides of the croquettes.

✤ Mix the 1 cup panko and cornmeal together. Dip croquettes into the 4 egg whites, then press into panko-cornmeal mixture. Pan-fry croquettes in oil until golden on each side. Drain on paper towels. Keep warm.

✤ Fan out 3 avocado slices on each plate and top with ¼ cup cabbage. Place 1 tablespoon aïoli at the base of each cabbage mound. Place a croquette on top of each dollop of aïoli. Garnish each plate with a lemon wedge and cilantro sprigs and serve.

SERVES FOUR

Marinated Cabbage

¼ cup rice wine vinegar
2 tablespoons sugar
1 cup red cabbage, finely shredded

✤ Combine the vinegar and sugar and whisk until the sugar is dissolved. Add the cabbage and mix well. Refrigerate.

MAKES 1 CUP

Jalapeño Aïoli

1 cup mayonnaise
½ teaspoon minced garlic
¼ teaspoon cayenne
1½ tablespoons minced jalapeño
¼ cup minced red onion
1 teaspoon grated lime zest
1 tablespoon chopped cilantro
¼ teaspoon kosher salt
Pinch of black pepper
Juice of ½ lime
½ teaspoon chile powder

✤ Mix all ingredients together well. Refrigerate for up to 4 days.

MAKES 1⅓ CUPS

Soy Ginger King Salmon

Michele Camera-Faurot, Cafe Michele

This simple recipe showcases the majesty of king salmon: full of flavor, exceptionally moist, and brimming with omega-3 fatty acids. This dish is lovely as the centerpiece of a tossed green salad.

1½-pound skinless king salmon fillet
½ cup sesame oil
⅓ cup soy sauce
3 tablespoons minced garlic
3 tablespoons minced fresh ginger
3 tablespoons Clarified Butter (page 203)

⚓ Cut the fillet into four equal portions. Place them in a single layer in a baking dish. Add the sesame oil. Gently turn the fillets so that they are each completely coated with the sesame oil. Cover the dish with plastic wrap and refrigerate for at least 2 hours or overnight. Remove the salmon from the refrigerator, add soy sauce, garlic, and ginger. Turn to coat as before. Cover and refrigerate for 1 hour. Heat clarified butter in a griddle or large sauté pan over medium heat. Add salmon to the griddle, skin side up. Cover and cook until the fish has cooked halfway up the side of the fillets. Turn the fillets over, cover, and cook until just done.

SERVES FOUR

Vodka-Cured Gravlax

Jack Amon, The Marx Bros. Cafe

Russian settlers had a great influence on Alaska, and that heritage is reflected in the dishes Alaska's chefs choose to show off outside of the state. This is an appetizer of Scandinavian/ Russian origin that Amon served at the James Beard House in New York City. Experiment with different types of fish cured in different toppings. Arctic char goes well with mint, and Copper River red salmon is nice with fennel.

3 pounds silver salmon fillet, skinned
¼ cup vodka
1 tablespoon crushed white peppercorns
½ cup roughly chopped dill
2 tablespoons kosher salt
2 tablespoons sugar
¼ cup Honey Mustard Sauce (recipe follows)
4 Potato Pancakes, quartered (recipe follows)
½ cup Sour Cream Dill Sauce (recipe follows)
¼ cup smoked salmon caviar
Sprigs of dill, for garnish

⁕ To make gravlax, coat the flesh of both sides of the salmon with the vodka and then the pepper. Place the salmon, skin side down, in a pan large enough to hold the fillet without bending. Sprinkle dill over salmon, then salt and sugar. Cover the salmon with aluminum foil and weigh it down with a board and a 5-pound weight. Refrigerate for 48 to 72 hours, turning the salmon and basting every 12 hours with accumulated juices.

⁕ Remove the salmon from the pan and pat dry. Wrap in plastic wrap and refrigerate until ready to serve (up to 2 days).

⁕ Thinly slice the gravlax on the diagonal, 3 to 4 slices per person. Roll the slices into 4 rose shapes. Set aside in refrigerator.

⁕ With a squirt bottle filled with honey mustard sauce, squeeze out a flower pattern with the sauce on each of 4 cold plates. Place a salmon rose on the sauce.

⁕ Arrange the potato pancake wedges around the salmon rose. Drizzle the pancakes with sour cream dill sauce. Sprinkle the caviar on top of the sauce. Garnish with dill sprigs.

SERVES FOUR

Honey Mustard Sauce

⅓ cup honey
1 tablespoon Dijon mustard
2 teaspoons finely chopped dill

✤ Combine all the ingredients and place in a squeeze bottle. Refrigerate.

MAKES ½ CUP

Sour Cream Dill Sauce

1 cup heavy cream
¼ cup sour cream
Juice of 1 lemon
1 tablespoon rice wine vinegar
3 tablespoons chopped dill
Freshly ground black pepper

✤ Combine all the ingredients and chill.

MAKES 1 ½ CUPS

Potato Pancakes

1 large boiling potato, peeled and coarsely grated
Juice of 1 lemon
2 tablespoons minced shallots
1 tablespoon minced garlic
2 tablespoons minced parsley
1 egg, beaten
2 tablespoons flour
¼ teaspoon salt
Pinch of ground black pepper
2 tablespoons vegetable oil

✤ Put the grated potato in a bowl with the lemon juice mixed with 2 cups water. Swirl, then drain and squeeze the potatoes dry.

✤ Mix the potatoes in the same bowl with the shallots, garlic, parsley, egg, flour, salt, and pepper. Heat a sauté pan over medium heat with the oil until the oil shimmers.

✢ For each pancake fry about ¼ cup of the mixture formed into a 2½-inch circle until it is browned on one side. Flip the pancake over and brown the other side. Drain on paper towels. Cut into wedges.

MAKES ABOUT SIX PANCAKES

Salmon Caviar

Alaskan chefs use the glistening orange-red eggs of salmon in many ways. The eggs can be eaten fresh, but many Alaskan chefs make their own caviar. The treated eggs are wonderful as a garnish for salmon dishes or served plain on good crackers with a little cream cheese or on the tips of endive leaves that have been painted with a little crème fraîche. The trick is to get the membrane separated from the eggs. Chefs use a variation of a basic method that involves breaking the egg sacs with their hands and separating the eggs into a bowl. Some chefs rub the sacs over a square of wire mesh with holes big enough for the eggs to drop through. The eggs sit for an hour or even or a day or two in a salt-water solution. Lemon, vodka, or soy sauce can be added to the brine. Some cooks use a little sugar or honey. A gentle rinse with fresh water and the caviar is ready to go.

—Kim Severson

Alaskan Weathervane Scallop Purses

Brett Custer, The Homestead Restaurant

When most cooks think of making a savory mousse, the panic sets in. Custer streamlines the task, creating a simple yet elegant appetizer or main course. Using large weathervane sea scallops is a treat, and this recipe preserves and showcases their delicacy.

RED PEPPER COULIS

1 red pepper, deseeded, deribbed, and chopped
½ teaspoon salt
¼ teaspoon white pepper
½ cup white wine

PORTOBELLO STUFFING

4 portobello mushrooms
2 tablespoons butter
½ teaspoon salt
¼ teaspoon pepper
2 cups heavy cream

SCALLOP MOUSSE

1 pound weathervane or other large sea scallops, tough muscle from sides removed
½ teaspoon salt
½ teaspoon ground white pepper
¼ teaspoon curry powder
1 cup heavy cream

SCALLOP PURSES

8 sheets phyllo pastry
6 tablespoons butter, melted, plus extra for greasing pan
16 green onion tops

⚜ To make the coulis, simmer red pepper, salt, white pepper, and wine for 30 minutes. Purée in a food processor. Reserve.

⚜ To make the portobello stuffing, preheat the oven to 350°F. Scrape the black gills from the bottom of the mushrooms with a teaspoon and finely chop the mushrooms. In an ovenproof pan, sauté mushrooms in the butter, stirring often, until most of the moisture is cooked out, about 13 minutes. Add salt, pepper, and cream; bring to a simmer. Place pan in oven and cook until cream is reduced and mixture thickens, about 30 minutes, stirring every 10 minutes. Allow stuffing to cool. Leave oven on.

✤ To make the scallop mousse, in a blender or food processor purée scallops, salt, white pepper, and curry powder until smooth, about 1 minute. Add cream and blend until smooth and fluffy, about 1 minute more.

✤ To make the scallop purses, divide one sheet of phyllo in half and brush halves with melted butter. Place one half on top of the other. Place an eighth of the portobello stuffing on the center of the phyllo sheet. Top with an eighth of the scallop mousse. Fold all corners of the phyllo up toward the center and tie with a green onion top. Repeat seven times. Place the eight purses on a lightly greased baking dish. Bake until golden brown, about 10 minutes. Remove cooked green onion and retie purses with a fresh green onion on each.

✤ To serve, divide the purses among 4 warm plates. Drizzle with coulis.

SERVES EIGHT AS AN APPETIZER OR FOUR AS AN ENTRÉE

Wild Mushroom Tart

Jack Amon, The Marx Bros. Cafe

Shaggy manes, morels, boletes, puffballs, and hedgehogs all grow in Southcentral Alaska. This is a very popular appetizer that can easily double as an entrée at lunch. You can sub-stitute a mix of different domestic mushrooms if you can't find wild mushrooms, but wild are best.

  2 tablespoons butter
  1 large onion, sliced thin
  1 tablespoon cider vinegar
  3 eggs
  ¼ cup whole milk
  ½ cup heavy cream
  ⅛ teaspoon salt
  ⅛ teaspoon white pepper
  ¼ teaspoon nutmeg, grated
  One 5-inch prebaked Tart Shell (recipe follows)
  ¼ cup (tightly packed) grated Gruyère or Swiss cheese
  4 ounces fresh wild mushrooms, sliced thin
  1 tablespoon chopped fresh thyme with flowers

- Preheat the oven to 350°F.

- Melt 1 tablespoon of the butter in a heavy skillet over medium-low heat. Add the onion and cook until light brown. Add the vinegar and continue cooking until light caramel color. Set aside.

- In a mixing bowl, gently whisk together the eggs, milk, and cream. Add the salt, pepper, and nutmeg and combine.

- Spread the caramelized onions evenly over the bottom of the baked tart shell. Cover with grated cheese, then mushrooms. Pour the egg mixture over the mush-rooms, being careful not to fill it over the lip of the shell. Sprinkle the thyme on top. Melt the remaining 1 tablespoon of butter and brush the mushrooms with it from time to time while the tart bakes. Bake 25 to 30 minutes, or until custard is just set.

SERVES FOUR

Tart Shell

½ cup flour
¼ teaspoon salt
¼ teaspoon sugar
3 tablespoons butter, chilled
1 egg yolk
1½ teaspoons sour cream

✣ Preheat the oven to 375°F.

✣ Mix together the flour, salt, and sugar. Add the butter. With a pastry cutter or 2 knives, cut the butter into the flour mixture until it resembles cornmeal. In a separate small bowl, mix together the egg yolk and sour cream. Add to flour mixture. Mix together until it is well blended and holds together. Press into a ball, wrap with plastic wrap, and refrigerate for at least 1 hour.

✣ Roll out until ⅛ inch thick, and place in a tart pan with a removable bottom. Prick the dough lightly with a fork. Fill with pastry weights or dried beans and bake for 10 minutes.

✣ Remove the weights and return to the oven for 5 minutes more, or until the crust is lightly browned.

MAKES ONE 5-INCH SHELL, ½ INCH DEEP

Soups, Salads, _and_ Sandwiches

Alaskan Seafood Chowder

Elizabeth King, Southside Bistro

In France, bouillabaisse is king. In San Francisco, the Italians perfected cioppino. In Alaska, warming fish chowders get people through the winter. Since there is usually a lot of seafood around Alaskan kitchens, this stew takes advantage of it. In this recipe, you can substitute whatever sort of sturdy fish might be available, but Alaskan salmon is best.

Chef King is an advocate of seasoning at every step. Don't wait until the very end to add salt and pepper. It will create more depth in flavor if you season as you go. Always add a little salt when sautéing vegetables. It will allow them to release their flavors to the fullest.

2 pounds Alaskan steamer clams, scrubbed

½ teaspoon salt

Pinch of freshly ground black pepper

1 tablespoon chopped garlic

1 tablespoon chopped shallots

2 cups steaming liquid, such as Fish Stock (page 197),
    white wine, or water

2 ribs celery, finely diced

1 white onion, finely diced

½ carrot, peeled, finely diced

2 cloves garlic, minced

2 shallots, minced

⅓ cup flour

1½ teaspoons chopped fresh thyme

1½ tablespoons chopped basil

1½ tablespoons chopped Italian parsley

¾ cup dry white wine

1 cup Fish Stock (page 197) or water

1½ cups heavy cream

1½ tablespoons fresh lemon juice

½ cup cooked sweet corn (fresh, canned, or frozen)

4 ounces Yukon Gold potatoes, diced small

8 ounces Alaskan salmon, diced small

Kosher salt, freshly ground black pepper, and cayenne

2 tablespoons snipped fresh chives

✦ Put the clams, salt, pepper, garlic, shallots, and steaming liquid in a large pot. Cover and steam over high heat until most of the clams have opened. Discard any unopened clams. Remove the clams and set aside the broth. When the clams are cool enough to handle, pick the clam meat out and set aside. Discard the clam shells.

✦ Melt the butter in a large soup pot over medium heat. Add the celery, onion, carrot, garlic, and shallots. Cook until the onions begin to get tender, about 6 minutes. Add the flour, stir well, and continue to cook over medium heat for about 2 minutes without browning the mixture. Add the wine and whisk in with a heavy whisk. Simmer for 2 minutes. Add the reserved clam broth, the fish stock, cream, and lemon juice. Bring to a simmer.

✦ Add the corn and potatoes. Simmer until the potatoes are tender, about 10 minutes. Add the salmon and reserved clams. Simmer 2 minutes longer. Adjust the seasoning with salt, pepper, and cayenne to taste. Garnish with chives and serve.

SERVES FOUR AS AN ENTRÉE OR SIX TO EIGHT AS A STARTER

Southside Black Bean Soup

Jens Nannestad, Southside Bistro

Alaska is a land of travelers and cultures. It isn't unheard of to find people from Latin American countries and the Caribbean who traveled north seeking fortune and adventure. Thus, the flavors of those countries don't seem out of place. This soup is almost always a sellout at the Bistro. Lime juice gives it extra brightness.

2 cups dried black beans
2 tablespoons vegetable oil
½ red onion, diced
½ white onion, diced
1 stalk celery, diced
2 tablespoons chopped garlic
2 tablespoons chopped shallots
3 tablespoons chopped cilantro
2 ripe tomatoes, chopped
2 tablespoons chopped green onion
1 jalapeño, seeded if desired, chopped
1 teaspoon ground dried chipotle chile
½ cup white wine
4 cups Chicken Stock (page 194) or canned chicken broth
Seasonings, such as ground coriander, ground cumin, chile powder,
    freshly ground black pepper, kosher salt, lemon juice, and lime juice

GARNISH

Salsa
Sour cream
Sprigs of cilantro
Fried tortilla strips

✧ Soak the beans in water for 24 hours. Drain and rinse.

✧ Heat the oil in a soup pot over medium-high heat. Sauté the onions and celery until just tender, about 5 minutes. Reduce the heat, add the garlic and shallots, and cook 1 minute. Add the beans, cilantro, tomatoes, green onion, jalapeño, chipotle, wine, and stock; bring to a simmer. Cook until the beans are tender, about 1 hour.

✤ Remove half of the soup and purée in a food processor. Return the puréed soup to the pot. Add seasonings to taste.

✤ Serve hot with garnishes of salsa, sour cream, cilantro sprigs, and fried tortilla strips.

SERVES TEN

The Ethnic Influence

On paper, Alaska doesn't seem ethnically diverse. Census data show almost two thirds of the population is Caucasian. But the state—and particularly its biggest city, Anchorage—is something of a cultural crossroads, and the influence of different culinary traditions is evident in the dishes served in many of Alaska's restaurants.

You'll find some of the nation's best sushi in Anchorage, partly because the city was a stopover for flights to and from the Far East. The state also enjoys relatively quick access to the fish of Hawaii and Japan. That, coupled with the pristine nature of Alaska's wild fish, make for superb sashimi and sushi.

And if you're in town, be sure to try some of the city's Korean restaurants. The city has a substantial Korean population, which began when Korean War veterans who had been stationed in Alaska married Korean women. Many moved back to Alaska, and families followed.

Even in small, rural towns the impact of immigrants can be seen. You can eat Vietnamese food in Dutch Harbor, Chinese food in Nome. In southeast Alaska you'll find strong Scandinavian influences in towns like Petersburg.

The sturdy food of Russia also has influenced the way Alaskans eat. Little Diomede Island off the west coast of Alaska is only 2.5 miles from Russia's Big Diomede Island and parts of the state were once under the Russian flag. Fish pies, potato dishes, cabbage salads, and preserved mushroom recipes all reflect that heritage.

The food of Alaska's Eskimo and Indian population, who make up about 17 percent of the state, is also reflected in the extensive use of wild berries and preserved fish. The myriad fish treatments on menus throughout the state echo methods of drying and smoking salmon and other fish that have been used by Native Alaskans for thousands of years.

—Kim Severson

Spicy Garnet Sweet Potato Soup with Alaskan King Crab

Laura Cole, 229 Parks Restaurant and Tavern

The common sweet potato reaches a new level with the addition of the royal member of the crustacean family. A hint of cayenne is a nice foil to the richness of the sweet potato.

> 1 tablespoon extra-virgin olive oil
> ¾ cup thinly sliced leeks (white and light green part only)
> 1 medium shallot, minced
> 2 cloves garlic, minced
> 2 cups washed, peeled, and diced garnet sweet potatoes
> 1 teaspoon minced fresh thyme
> ¼ teaspoon cayenne (less, if desired)
> 2 tablespoons light- to medium-amber maple syrup
> 3 cups crab or lobster stock (see page 199)
> 1 to 2 cups whole milk
> Sea salt and freshly ground black pepper
> 2 cups king crab, picked over
> ¼ cup chopped cilantro
> Tortilla chips or crisped tortilla strips

✦ In a large sauté pan heat the olive oil over medium heat. Add leeks and shallot; cook, stirring, until tender, about 4 minutes. Add garlic; stir to coat with oil. Add sweet potatoes; stir to coat with oil. Add thyme and cayenne; stir to coat with oil. Add maple syrup; stir to mix well. Add crab stock and bring to a simmer. Simmer, covered, until sweet potatoes are tender, about 45 minutes. Remove from heat and purée in a blender or food processor, adding milk a small amount at a time to reach desired flavor and consistency. Season with salt and pepper.

✦ To serve, divide soup among 4 warm bowls. Mound ½ cup crab in the center of each bowl. Garnish with cilantro and tortilla chips.

SERVES FOUR

Homestead Potato and Two-Cheese Soup

Brett Custer, The Homestead Restaurant

This soup is just what the doctor ordered. Simple, clean, with the hook of Scottish beer. Any beer will work, but a local microbrew will certainly raise the flavor a notch. Be sure to remove the soup from the heat before stirring in the cheese, as high heat causes cheese to become grainy.

1 tablespoon canola oil

¼ cup finely diced carrots

½ cup finely diced yellow onion

¼ teaspoon cayenne

3 cloves garlic, minced

3½ cups unsalted Chicken Stock (page 194) or Vegetable Stock (page 196)

1 cup Homer Brewing Company Red Knot Scottish Ale

2 Anaheim chilies, roasted, peeled, and finely diced

1½ cups cooked, mashed russet potato

½ cup heavy cream

4 ounces cooked chopped chorizo sausage (optional)

2 ounces (¾ cup) shredded sharp white cheddar

2 ounces (¾ cup) shredded smoked mozzarella

Salt and freshly ground black pepper

⚓ Heat the canola oil in a large soup pot over medium-high heat until it shimmers. Add carrots, onion, and cayenne and sauté until the onion softens, about 6 minutes. Add garlic, sauté for 15 seconds, then add chicken stock and beer; bring to a simmer. Add chilies and potato. Simmer soup, stirring often, for 30 minutes. Remove from heat, add cream, chorizo (if using), cheddar, and mozzarella. Stir until the cheeses melt. Season with salt and pepper. Serve in warm bowls.

SERVES FOUR

Onion Borscht

Kirsten Dixon, Within the Wild Lodges

Russian food is a favorite topic of Dixon's. Russian explorers were the first known white men to set foot in Alaska in 1741. They set up the first non-Native towns and trading centers. More than a century later, the United States bought Alaska from Russia for $7.2 million. With all that history, food with Russian influences makes sense on Alaskan tables. Dixon respects the history, but she also has lots of easy-to-store beets and onions on hand— essential elements of Russian cooking. This is her loose interpretation of borscht. It is meant to be a first-course accompaniment to a heavy meal such as beef tenderloin.

3 large beets, scrubbed

4 tablespoons (½ stick) butter

Salt and freshly ground black pepper

2¾ cups Rich Beef Broth (recipe follows)

2 medium-size sweet onions (such as Vidalia), peeled

1 teaspoon freshly grated nutmeg

1 tablespoon chopped fresh oregano

¼ cup sour cream

✤ Preheat the oven to 400°F.

✤ Rub the beets with 2 tablespoons of the butter and sprinkle with salt and pepper. Wrap the beets individually in aluminum foil and place them on a small baking pan large enough to hold them comfortably. Add ¼ cup of the beef broth diluted with a little water to the bottom of the pan. Place the pan in the center of the oven and bake for 1 hour, or until the beets are tender. Set aside to cool.

✤ Quarter the onions, liberally salt and pepper them, and spread with the remaining 2 tablespoons butter. Place the onions in a small baking dish large enough to hold them comfortably. Sprinkle the onions with nutmeg and oregano. Add enough of the remaining beef broth to cover the bottom of the pan. Cover with aluminum foil and place in the center of the oven and bake until tender, about 20 minutes.

✤ Remove the skin of the beets by rubbing with paper or cloth towel. Chop 1 beet into small dice and quarter the remaining two.

- Place the remaining 2½ cups beef broth in a medium saucepan over medium heat. Add the diced beet. Reduce the heat and simmer for 10 minutes. Strain the broth, discarding diced beet.

- To serve, place 2 onion quarters and 2 beet quarters into each of 4 warmed wide-rimmed shallow bowls. Divide the hot broth among the bowls. Serve the sour cream on the side.

    SERVES FOUR

Rich Beef Broth

> ¼ cup vegetable oil
> 2 pounds beef bones, cut into ½-inch lengths
> ¾ cup chopped onion
> ½ cup chopped carrot
> ½ cup chopped celery
> 2 quarts Beef Stock (page 195)
> 1 small leek, white and light green part, thinly sliced

- Preheat the oven to 400°F.

- Pour oil into a small roasting pan and place in oven for 10 minutes. Add bones, toss, and roast until browned all over, about 20 minutes. Add onion, carrot, and celery. Roast for another 10 minutes.

- Remove bones and vegetables from the roasting pan and place in a saucepan. Discard remaining oil in the pan. Add 1 cup of stock to the pan. With a wooden spoon, scrape up any brown bits in the roasting pan and add the stock–brown bit mixture and the leek to the saucepan.

- Over medium-high heat, bring the broth to a simmer. Adjust heat to maintain a simmer and cook for 4 hours. Strain broth; discard solids.

- If not using broth immediately, cool in an ice bath. Refrigerate for up to 2 days or freeze for a later use.

    MAKES 1 QUART

Potato–Green Chile Soup

JoAnn Asher, Sacks Cafe

Like cooking in much of the rest of the country, Alaska's cuisine went through a Southwest phase. This soup originally came out of the period in the late 1980s and early 1990s when the chiles, cumin, and other flavors from Arizona and New Mexico were common. It remains a favorite at Sacks Cafe, even though it doesn't turn up on the menu as much as it used to. Still, people always ask for the recipe when it does.

4 medium potatoes, peeled and cubed
3½ cups Chicken Stock (page 194) or Vegetable Stock (page 196)
1 tablespoon butter
1 tablespoon olive oil
1 cup diced onion
½ cup diced red pepper
1 teaspoon minced garlic
1 teaspoon salt
½ teaspoon ground cumin
1 teaspoon dried oregano
1 teaspoon ground coriander
¾ cup half-and-half
⅓ cup diced canned green chiles
¼ cup grated sharp cheddar
¼ cup grated Monterey Jack

✧ Cover the potatoes with stock in a large saucepan, bring to a simmer, and cook until the potatoes are tender. Process in a food processor until the potatoes are puréed. Return the potato-stock mixture to the saucepan and keep warm.

✧ Heat the butter and oil in a skillet over medium heat until they sizzle. Add the onion, red pepper, and garlic and cook until the onion and pepper are soft. Add the salt, cumin, oregano, and coriander. Add the onion mixture to the potato mixture and mix well. Add the half-and-half and chiles. Taste and adjust the seasonings.

✧ Heat the soup until it steams, then divide among 4 hot soup bowls. Garnish with cheeses and serve.

SERVES FOUR

Shellfish Portuguese

Brett Custer, The Homestead Restaurant

Following the global tradition of coastal cookery, Custer hits a home run with his adaptation of shellfish stew, using the bounty of Alaskan waters. Any local mollusks would work well in this recipe, as would different types of spicy sausage.

2 hard Spanish chorizo sausages
2 teaspoons olive oil
1 pound fresh mussels, rinsed and debearded
1 pound fresh littleneck clams, rinsed
1 tablespoon minced garlic
1 tablespoon minced shallot
4 tablespoons (½ stick) butter
1 cup white wine
1 cup Fish Stock (page 197)
¼ cup Red Pepper Coulis (page 27)
¼ cup julienned red pepper
¼ cup julienned red onion
4 dashes Tabasco
2 pinches of salt
2 pinches of pepper
3 ounces (1 cup) shredded Asiago

⚓ Sauté the sausages in olive oil until they start to brown, about 6 minutes; cut into 2-inch pieces. Combine the sausages, mussels, clams, garlic, shallot, butter, wine, fish stock, red pepper coulis, red pepper, red onion, Tabasco, salt, and pepper in a shallow pan, cover, and simmer over medium heat, tossing occasionally until the mussels and clams have opened, about 6 minutes. Discard any unopened mussels and clams. Divide between two bowls. Sprinkle with cheese.

SERVES TWO

Ginger Carrot Bisque with Cilantro Yogurt

Brett Knipmeyer, Kinley's

This soup is a real winner. It is simple to make but elegant in flavor and presentation.

GINGER CARROT BISQUE

1 tablespoon butter
½ cup sliced yellow onion
1¼ pounds medium carrots, peeled and chopped
1 rounded tablespoon minced garlic
2 tablespoons minced fresh ginger
3½ cups Vegetable Stock (page 196)
One 5.6-ounce can coconut milk
Scant pinch of ground cardamom
Pinch of ground cloves
Salt and freshly ground black pepper

CILANTRO YOGURT

½ cup chopped cilantro
½ cup plain yogurt

GARNISH

4 sprigs of cilantro

⚓ To make the bisque, melt the butter in a soup pot, add onion and carrots, and cook over medium heat until onions are soft, about 6 minutes. Add garlic and ginger, cook 15 seconds, add vegetable stock, bring to a simmer. Simmer bisque until carrots are soft. Purée bisque with an immersion blender or in a food processor. Stir in coconut milk, cardamom, and cloves. Return bisque to a simmer. Season with salt and pepper.

⚓ To make the cilantro yogurt, combine the chopped cilantro and yogurt. Purée with an immersion blender or in a food processor.

⚓ Divide the bisque among 4 warm soup bowls. Place a dollop of yogurt on the bisque and top with a cilantro sprig.

SERVES FOUR

Cream of Alaskan Summer Squash and Fresh Sweet Basil Soup

Jens Nannestad, Southside Bistro

Summer is short, but the days are long. Thus, gardeners experience amazing results with squash, lettuce, and peas. And as for gardeners everywhere, too much zucchini can be a problem. This soup makes the best of the situation. The fresh basil really highlights the vegetables.

2 tablespoons olive oil
2 large zucchini, diced
2 large yellow squash, diced
½ red onion, diced
½ white onion, diced
2 ribs celery, diced
2 tablespoons chopped garlic
1 cup white wine
3 cups Chicken Stock (page 194) or canned chicken broth
2 cups heavy cream
½ cup chopped basil
Seasonings, such as kosher salt, freshly ground black pepper, crushed red pepper, cayenne
¼ cup pistachio nuts, toasted and roughly chopped

✤ Heat the olive oil in a soup pot over medium heat. Add the zucchini, yellow squash, onions, celery, and garlic and stir. Cover and cook for 5 to 10 minutes without browning any of the vegetables. Add the wine, stock, and cream and simmer for 30 minutes.

✤ Purée the soup in a food processor, return to the pot, and heat over medium heat until hot. Whisk in the basil and add seasonings to your liking.

✤ Divide among 4 large, warm soup bowls. Garnish with pistachios and serve.

SERVES FOUR

Van's Famous Caesar Salad

Van Hale, The Marx Bros. Cafe

This salad was first prepared at Caesar Cardini's restaurant in Tijuana in the late 1920s. Its popularity grew and today the Caesar salad is an American institution. The version made tableside by the Marx Bros. Cafe's wine steward, Van Hale, is simple. Some versions call for mustard and Worcestershire sauce to jazz it up. Van just uses the finest vinegar, olive oil, anchovies, and imported Parmesan cheese.

To make the salad, a good wooden bowl is essential. Season the bowl well with olive oil and never wash it with soap.

2 eggs, at room temperature
2 teaspoons plus ¼ cup extra-virgin olive oil
6 garlic cloves
6 anchovy fillets
1 lemon
1 teaspoon aged balsamic vinegar
2 tablespoons freshly grated Parmigiano-Reggiano
2 large heads of romaine lettuce, washed, torn, and spun dry
1 cup croutons
Freshly ground black pepper

⚜ Bring a small pan of water to a boil. Add the eggs and boil 1 minute to coddle them. Remove the eggs from the water and set aside.

⚜ Drizzle the 2 teaspoons olive oil in the bottom of a large wooden bowl. Add the garlic and mash it well with a fork. Add the anchovies and continue to mash until the mixture resembles a fine paste. Using a wooden spoon, mash the garlic-anchovy mixture into the sides and bottom of the bowl.

⚜ Break the coddled eggs into the bowl, add the juice of the lemon, and mix thoroughly. Add the ¼ cup olive oil and the vinegar and blend.

⚜ Add the Parmigiano. Add the lettuce and toss the leaves so that they are coated with dressing. Add the croutons and mix well.

⚜ Serve on a chilled plate and garnish with a sprinkle of Parmigiano and a grind of cracked pepper.

SERVES FOUR

Matanuska Valley Summer Beet Salad

Michele Camera-Faurot, Cafe Michele

The Matanuska Valley is the market basket for south-central Alaska. Although better known for 50-pound cabbages and 5-pound zucchini, the valley yields a superb variety of produce in the summer. Michele uses organically grown Cylindra and golden beets from Wolverine Farms in Palmer.

3 medium Cylindra beets, peeled and chopped into ½-inch dice
3 medium golden beets, peeled and chopped into ½-inch dice
⅓ cup olive oil
¼ cup chopped fresh oregano
Salt and freshly ground black pepper
4 cups mesclun greens
¾ cup local organic feta

✧ Preheat the oven to 400°F. In a medium bowl, mix the beets with olive oil and oregano. Season lightly with salt and pepper (check the feta you will use for saltiness). Spread the beet mixture on a parchment-paper-covered baking pan. Roast the beets for 12 to 15 minutes (they should be al dente). Remove beets and allow them to cool to room temperature. Divide the greens among 4 salad plates and top with beets. Sprinkle with crumbled feta.

SERVES FOUR

Escalope of Alaskan Salmon With Chive and Lime Salad

Al Levinsohn, Kincaid Grill

Salmon is so common that Alaskan chefs have a field day creating new ways to use it. Here, an interesting mix of deep-fried potato croutons and lots of crunchy daikon radish and bell pepper give this hot salad a lively texture.

CITRUS VINAIGRETTE

2 tablespoons orange juice concentrate

2 tablespoons fresh lime juice

2 tablespoons honey

1 tablespoons rice vinegar

1 cup olive oil

Salt and freshly ground black pepper

POTATO CROUTONS

1 baking potato, peeled

Vegetable oil, for frying

Salt and freshly ground black pepper

CHIVE AND LIME SALAD

½ medium red bell pepper, sliced thin

½ medium yellow bell pepper, sliced thin

½ cup thinly sliced red onion

2 limes, peeled and sliced thin

½ cup bean sprouts

½ cup daikon sprouts

½ cup thinly sliced daikon root

½ cup chopped cilantro

2 tablespoons minced fresh chives

2 cups mesclun or spring greens mix

SALMON

4 salmon fillets, 5 ounces each

Salt and ground white pepper

1 tablespoon olive oil

- To prepare the vinaigrette, place the orange juice concentrate, lime juice, honey, and rice vinegar in a blender. With the blender running slowly, add the oil in a thin, steady stream.

- Season with salt and pepper to taste. Refrigerate.

- To prepare the potato croutons, dice enough potato to make ½ cup. Deep-fry in vegetable oil until crisp and golden. Drain, season with salt and pepper, and keep warm.

- For the salad, toss together the red and yellow peppers, onion, limes, bean sprouts, daikon sprouts, daikon root, cilantro, and chives in a medium bowl.

- Wash the mesclun mix, drain, and dry.

- Season the salmon fillets with salt and pepper. Heat the olive oil in a skillet over medium-high heat until it shimmers. Pan-fry the salmon until it is just cooked through, a few minutes per side, depending on thickness.

- Add 2 tablespoons of the vinaigrette to the lettuce and toss to coat. Divide the salad among 4 plates. Place a salmon fillet on top of each plate of lettuce.

- Add ¼ cup of vinaigrette to the bowl of vegetables and toss to coat. Divide vegetables and place an equal amount on top of each salmon fillet. Season with salt and pepper.

- Drizzle the remaining 2 tablespoons of vinaigrette around the edges of the salads. Top with croutons and serve.

SERVES FOUR

Kinley's White Salad

Brett Knipmeyer, Kinley's

In the middle of an Alaskan winter, when local green vegetables are nonexistent, this salad showcases vegetables that are often ignored in the summer. Also, you'll never have to buy premade blue cheese dressing again.

BLUE CHEESE DRESSING

2 tablespoons white wine vinegar

1 cup high-quality mayonnaise

1 cup sour cream

½ teaspoon Worcestershire sauce

Dash Tabasco

6 ounces blue cheese

Heavy cream

Salt and freshly ground black pepper

WHITE SALAD

½ cup leeks, washed and cut into ¼-inch thick circles

1 cup small cauliflower florets

½ cup peeled and finely diced celeriac (celery root)

1 cup peeled and finely diced parsnips

1 cup peeled and finely diced rutabaga

½ cup thinly sliced fennel bulb

1 cup canned artichoke hearts, rinsed

Salt and freshly ground black pepper

4 cups baby mesclun greens

GARNISH

Blue cheese crumbles

⚜ To make the blue cheese dressing, purée the vinegar, mayonnaise, sour cream, Worcestershire, Tabasco, and 2 ounces of the blue cheese until smooth. Remove to a container and fold in the remaining blue cheese. Adjust consistency with cream, season with salt and pepper, and refrigerate.

✦ To make the salad, blanch the leeks, cauliflower, celeriac, parsnips, and ruta-baga in simmering water for 1 minute, drain, shock in ice water, and drain again. Remove to a large bowl, and add fennel and artichoke hearts. Fold in 1 cup of the blue cheese dressing. Season with salt and pepper.

✦ To serve, divide the mesclun greens among 4 plates. Place a quarter of the white salad mixture on each plate. Garnish with blue cheese crumbles.

SERVES FOUR

Grilled Summer Vegetable Salad with Goat Cheese and Pine Nuts

Elizabeth King, Southside Bistro

King, the chef de cuisine at Southside Bistro, created this Mediterranean-style salad to take advantage of late summer's zucchini and squash harvest. Use any good-quality goat cheese. It really stands up to the grilled vegetables.

2 cloves garlic, minced

2 tablespoons thinly sliced basil

1 tablespoon chopped Italian parsley

2 teaspoons minced fresh oregano

¼ cup balsamic vinegar

¼ cup extra-virgin olive oil

Kosher salt and freshly ground black pepper

1 medium zucchini, cut lengthwise into ¼-inch slices

1 medium yellow squash, cut lengthwise into ¼-inch slices

1 medium red onion, cut into ¼-inch slices

1 pound fresh asparagus, tough ends removed

½ pound mushrooms, halved

1 roasted red pepper (see page 52), peeled, seeded, and cut into thin strips

Olive oil

¼ cup pine nuts, toasted

5 ounces goat cheese

✤ Preheat the grill.

✤ Make a vinaigrette in a large bowl by whisking together the garlic, basil, parsley, oregano, vinegar, and olive oil. Season with salt and pepper.

✤ Prepare the zucchini, yellow squash, onion, asparagus, and mushrooms by rubbing them with a little olive oil and seasoning with salt and pepper. Place the vegetables on the grill and mark them before turning. Cook the vegetables until they just begin to get tender, not mushy. The red onions and asparagus will tend to cook more quickly than the others. As the grilled vegetables are done, place them in the vinaigrette with the roasted red peppers and toss to coat.

✧ When all of the vegetables are finished cooking, divide the mixture among 4 large bowls. Sprinkle the pine nuts and goat cheese on top.

SERVES FOUR

Roasted Peppers

To roast peppers, rub the peppers lightly with olive oil and roast in a 400°F oven or on a grill over high heat. Cook until the skin is blistered lightly but do not char completely (this will make them bitter). Turn the peppers to cook on all sides evenly. When blistered on all sides, put the peppers in a bowl and cover tightly with plastic wrap or place in a plastic bag and seal. This will trap in moisture and allow the skin of the pepper to gently steam. Cool the pepper at room temperature for at least 15 minutes. Peel off the skin with a paring knife and remove all seeds and white ribs from inside.

—Glenn Denkler

Wildberry Salmon Salad

Kirsten Dixon, Within the Wild Lodges

This is an elegant little summer salad that Dixon serves at Within the Wild Lodges. She dresses salads with grapeseed oil and a little bit of walnut oil. She also prefers the proper salt and pepper for salads, using fleur de sel or Brittany sea salt and a house pepper mix of black peppercorns, white peppercorns, and allspice.

For the salmon, trim the sides of a fillet so there is a center cut of even thickness about three or four inches across. Red, or sockeye salmon, is Dixon's favorite for salads. Sometimes she marinates cherry tomatoes in balsamic or fig balsamic vinegar, sprinkles them with sea salt, and tosses them into the salad at the last minute.

> 4 center-cut Alaskan red salmon fillets, 4 ounces each
> Salt and freshly ground black pepper
> ½ cup grapeseed oil
> 6 cups mixed baby green lettuces
> ¼ cup walnut oil
> ¼ cup dried cherries
> ¼ cup fresh berries, such as blueberries or raspberries
> ½ small red onion, diced
> 2 ounces Danish blue cheese, cut into 4 slices

✦ Chill 4 salad plates.

✦ Season the salmon fillets with salt and pepper. Heat a medium sauté pan over medium-high heat. Add 1 tablespoon grapeseed oil to the pan and heat until it shimmers. Place 2 fillets, presentation side down, in the pan without crowding and sear for about 2½ minutes. Turn the fillets over and sear the other side for about 2½ minutes more. Remove and keep warm. Repeat with the other 2 fillets.

✦ Put the greens in a large bowl and toss with just enough grapeseed oil to coat the greens lightly. Drizzle with the walnut oil and toss. The amounts of oil necessary depend on the types of greens used. Lightly season the greens with salt and pepper.

✦ Place 1½ cups of the dressed greens on the center of each plate. Place a piece of warm salmon on top. Sprinkle the cherries, fresh berries, and red onion around the salad. Top with the blue cheese and serve.

SERVES FOUR

Cobb Salad Sandwich

Farrokh Larijani, Glacier BrewHouse

Leave it to an Alaskan to take a relaxed approach to the traditional. The classic American salad, invented in the late 1920s by Bob Cobb, manager of the original Brown Derby in Hollywood, California, is a fixture on many menus. Larijani took the classic and gave it an Alaskan twist. The radish salad provides a crisp and refreshing finish.

DIJON MAYONNAISE

1 cup bottled mayonnaise
¼ cup Dijon mustard
2 ounces Danish blue cheese, crumbled
¾ teaspoon freshly ground black pepper

SANDWICH

8 slices sourdough bread
8 ounces sliced honey baked ham
8 ounces sliced smoked turkey
8 pepper bacon slices, cooked crisp
2 cups iceberg lettuce, shredded
1¼ cups Radish Salad (recipe follows)
½ ripe avocado, sliced ⅛ inch thick
4 Roma tomatoes, cored and sliced

⚜ To prepare the dijon mayonnaise, combine all the ingredients. Refrigerate.

⚜ To make the sandwiches, toast the bread slices lightly and spread with some of the mayonnaise.

⚜ Fold each of the ham and turkey slices and layer them on the bread. Lay the bacon on top of the sliced meat. Top with lettuce, radish salad, avocado slices, and tomatoes and serve.

SERVES FOUR

Radish Salad

10 small radishes of any sort, scrubbed and sliced ⅛ inch thick

½ cup sliced (⅛ inch) red onions

1 cup sliced (⅛ inch) English cucumber

¼ cup rice wine vinegar

2 teaspoons sugar

⚜ Combine all ingredients and mix well. Refrigerate before serving.

SERVES FOUR TO SIX

Oyster Po'boys with Green Onion–Chipotle Aïoli

Brett Custer, The Homestead Restaurant

When fresh oysters are in season, the population of Homer rejoices. This is a fun way to enjoy one of the crown jewels of Alaskan seafood.

GREEN ONION–CHIPOTLE AÏOLI

2 green onions, roughly chopped

1½ teaspoons ground chipotle pepper

2 teaspoons minced garlic

3 egg yolks

1 teaspoon fresh lemon juice

1½ cups olive oil

Salt and freshly ground black pepper

OYSTER PO'BOYS

Peanut oil for frying

2 eggs

2 cups milk

2 cups panko (Japanese bread crumbs, available in Asian markets and some supermarkets)

½ teaspoon powdered garlic

1 tablespoon dry parsley

24 oysters, freshly shucked

1 cup flour

4 sourdough po'boy buns or steak rolls

3 cups shredded romaine lettuce

12 slices ripe tomato

⚜ To make the aïoli, in a food processor, mix the green onions, chipotle, minced garlic, egg yolks, and lemon juice with 1 tablespoon of the olive oil for 30 seconds. With the processor running, add the remaining oil in a slow drizzle. Season with salt and pepper and reserve. Leftovers may be kept refrigerated for up to 4 days.

⚜ To make the po'boys, add ½ inch peanut oil to a pan and heat over medium-high heat until it shimmers. Whisk the eggs and milk together in a bowl. In a separate bowl, blend the panko, powdered garlic, and parsley. Dredge the oysters in the flour and pat out excess. Dip the oysters first in the egg mixture, then the panko mixture. Pan-fry the oysters until golden on each side (no more than 2 minutes total). Drain on paper towels.

✢ To serve, lightly toast the po'boy buns. Place 6 oysters on each bun. Top with lettuce and tomato slices. Drizzle with aïoli.

SERVES FOUR

Entrées

Alaskan Seafood Gumbo

Al Levinsohn, Kincaid Grill

If you can't get Alaskan seafood, this dish allows you to use whatever fish or shellfish might look good at the market. The most difficult part of making a proper gumbo is the cooking of the roux (the mixture of oil and flour that is the thickening agent), which needs to be cooked to the color of an old penny. The trick is not to burn it. If you see black specks in the roux, you will have to repeat the step. Use patience and a long-handled wooden spoon to stir it while cooking so that you don't splatter hot roux on your hands.

½ teaspoon ground white pepper
½ teaspoon cayenne
½ teaspoon freshly ground black pepper
½ teaspoon dried thyme
½ teaspoon dried oregano
4 bay leaves
1 teaspoon kosher salt
¾ cup vegetable oil
¾ cup flour
1 cup diced onion
½ cup diced celery
½ cup diced green bell pepper
1 pound andouille sausage or kielbasa
5 cups Fish Stock (page 197)
1 pound assorted seafood, such as shrimp, crab, salmon, halibut, clams, and mussels
4 cups cooked long-grain rice
4 green onions, thinly sliced

⊹ Combine the white pepper, cayenne, black pepper, thyme, oregano, bay leaves, and salt and set aside.

⊹ Heat the oil in a large heavy-duty pot (preferably cast iron) over medium-high heat until it shimmers. Whisk in the flour until smooth. Stir the roux constantly until you obtain the proper brown color. As the roux darkens, reduce the heat to to medium to help protect it from burning.

+ Add the onion, celery, green pepper, and andouille and cook over medium heat until the vegetables are soft. Add 1½ teaspoons of the reserved seasoning, stir, and remove the pan from the heat.

+ Add stock carefully (it will sizzle as it touches the hot roux mixture). Let sit for 2 minutes, then incorporate by whisking it in. Return the pot to the stove and bring to a simmer. Cook gently for 30 minutes. Adjust the flavor with the seasoning and more salt if desired. Just prior to service, stir in seafood and cook until just done.

+ Divide the rice equally among 4 warm bowls and ladle the gumbo over. Garnish with green onions.

SERVES FOUR AS AN ENTRÉE OR EIGHT AS AN APPETIZER

Alder-Plank-Roasted Salmon

Jens Hansen, Jens' Restaurant

Native Americans have used this cooking method for thousands of years. Hansen used to prepare both fish and meat this way when he first started cooking in Alaska in the 1960s, but stopped for other, more "in" ways. It is making a comeback. He does not recommend using the same plank for meat and fish, as flavors set in. To clean the plank, hand–wash and rub it lightly with mineral oil. It should last for your lifetime.

1½ pounds salmon fillet, skin on
1 pound Plugrá or other European-style butter
½ cup chopped fresh dill
2 tablespoons fresh lemon juice
½ cup chopped dried berries
1 tablespoon crushed pepper mélange (mixture of black, white, green, and pink peppercorns)
3 tablespoons vegetable oil
1 alder plank

✢ Preheat the oven to 400°F.

✢ Trim and scale the salmon. Remove the pin bones with tweezers or needle-nosed pliers. Cut the salmon into 4 fillets. Make ⅛-inch cuts through the skin (not into red meat) about 1 inch apart.

✢ Place the butter, dill, lemon juice, berries, and pepper mélange in a mixing bowl and beat until light and fluffy. Set aside.

✢ Add the oil to a sauté pan large enough to hold the fillets and heat over medium-high heat until the oil shimmers. Sear the fillets, skin side down, for 30 seconds, then remove. Place the fillets, skin side up, on the alder plank. Smear equal portions of the butter mixture evenly over the salmon fillets. Roast the salmon for 8 minutes or until cooked to your likeness.

✢ Present the salmon on the plank straight from the oven.

SERVES FOUR

Ancho-Encrusted Alaskan Scallops with Angel Hair Pasta in Cilantro Pesto

Mike Holman, Sacks Cafe

Big, meaty sea scallops from Kodiak are best. In any case, ask your fishmonger for what are called hand-harvested or diver scallops.

CILANTRO PESTO

½ cup toasted slivered almonds

⅓ cup canola oil

¼ cup extra-virgin olive oil

½ cup chopped cilantro

2 green onions, chopped

1 to 2 jalapeños, seeded and chopped

2 cloves garlic, minced

2 tablespoons fresh lime juice

½ teaspoon salt

SCALLOPS

16 Alaskan sea scallops

1 tablespoon ancho chile powder

½ teaspoon sea salt

1 teaspoon dried oregano

1 teaspoon ground cumin

1 teaspoon ground coriander

2 tablespoons vegetable oil

PRESENTATION

½ red bell pepper, cut into ⅛-inch dice

½ yellow or orange bell pepper, cut into ⅛-inch dice

2 jalapeños, seeded and cut into ⅛-inch dice

1 teaspoon minced garlic

Pinch of salt

¼ pound angel hair pasta

✢ To make the pesto, purée all the ingredients in a food processor or blender. Check for salt to taste.

✣ To prepare the scallops, rinse the scallops and remove any attaching membrane. Combine the ancho powder, salt, oregano, cumin, and coriander.

✣ Press both sides of each scallop into the mixture. Pour the oil in a skillet and heat over medium heat until it shimmers. Sear each side of the scallops, removing just before they are cooked completely through, 1 minute or so on each side.

✣ To make the garnish, combine all the ingredients and set aside.

✣ Cook the pasta in salted water until al dente. Drain.

✣ Combine the pesto with the pasta and divide among 4 plates. Arrange 4 cooked scallops on top of each plate of pasta. Sprinkle the garnish on top and serve.

SERVES FOUR

Balsamic-Glazed Kodiak Scallops with Tomato Salsa

Elizabeth King, Southside Bistro

The crew at the Southside Bistro has a way with scallops. The trick is searing them in a hot pan or over a hot grill and cooking them only long enough to turn the outside opaque. The inside will continue to cook for a few moments, making the inner flesh just a step past rare—the perfect stage for a scallop. Saffron Risotto Cakes (page 171) are a wonderful accompaniment to this dish.

TOMATO SALSA

8 ounces vine-ripened tomatoes, finely diced

2 tablespoons finely diced red onion

3 tablespoons basil, cut into very thin strips

2 tablespoons parsley, chopped

1 clove garlic, minced

1 tablespoon extra-virgin olive oil

2 tablespoons balsamic vinegar

Salt and freshly ground black pepper

SCALLOPS

1½ cups balsamic vinegar

⅓ cup sugar

1½ pounds Kodiak scallops or other large sea scallops

Wooden skewers, soaked in water

Olive oil

Salt and freshly ground black pepper

✣ To make the salsa, combine the tomatoes, red onion, basil, parsley, garlic, olive oil, and 2 tablespoons balsamic vinegar in a large bowl. Season with salt and pepper to taste. Set the salsa aside.

✣ Simmer the 1½ cups balsamic vinegar and the sugar in a small saucepan until reduced by a third. Allow mixture to cool at room temperature.

✦ Preheat the grill until very hot. Skewer the scallops so that they are easier to handle on the grill. Brush the scallops with olive oil and season with 2 teaspoons salt and ¼ teaspoon pepper, or more to taste. Grill the scallops for 1 to 2 minutes on each side, or sauté the scallops in olive oil.

✦ Arrange the scallops on warm plates and drizzle with balsamic glaze. Garnish with tomato salsa.

SERVES FOUR

Grilled King Salmon on Tasso Cornbread with Blueberry Barbecue Sauce

Brett Knipmeyer, Kinley's

Tasso ham is a accompaniment found throughout Cajun and Creole recipes. Not really a ham, tasso does not come from the leg of the pig, but rather the shoulder (butt). The shoulder is sliced thinly, briefly cured, rinsed, rubbed with Cajun seasoning, then hot-smoked. The elegance of the salmon makes a very unusual—but satisfying—surf and turf when combined with tasso cornbread.

BLUEBERRY BARBECUE SAUCE

½ cup diced onion

2 teaspoons minced garlic

1 tablespoon canola oil

3 tablespoons red wine vinegar

2 teaspoons brown sugar

1 tablespoon honey

¼ cup Beef Stock (page 195)

⅓ cup ketchup

1 teaspoon dry mustard

1½ teaspoons Worcestershire sauce

1 cup blueberries

TASSO CORNBREAD

3 tablespoons canola oil

5 ounces tasso ham, diced

1 cup diced yellow onion

¾ cup diced red bell pepper

¾ cup yellow cornmeal

¾ cup all-purpose flour

2 teaspoons baking powder

1 teaspoon baking soda

¾ teaspoon salt

2 tablespoons granulated sugar

¾ cup buttermilk

1 egg

4 tablespoons (½ stick) butter, melted

GRILLED KING SALMON

4 king salmon fillets (6 ounces each)
Salt and freshly ground black pepper

✢ To make the barbecue sauce, in a large pan over medium heat cook the onion and garlic in canola oil until the onions are soft (don't brown), about 6 minutes. Add vinegar, brown sugar, honey, beef stock, ketchup, mustard, Worcestershire sauce, and blueberries. Simmer for 30 minutes.

✢ To make the cornbread, preheat the oven to 375°F. Put 2 tablespoons of the canola oil in an 8-inch square baking dish; place in oven. In a skillet, cook the tasso ham, onion, and pepper over medium heat in the remaining oil until the onion is translucent, about 12 minutes; transfer to a large bowl. Add cornmeal, flour, baking powder, baking soda, salt, and sugar. Mix with whisk to combine well. In another bowl, whip together buttermilk, egg, and melted butter. Fold buttermilk mixture into cornmeal mixture until just combined. Remove preheated baking dish from oven, add batter, and bake for 20 minutes.

✢ To make the salmon, preheat a grill until very hot. Season salmon with salt and pepper and grill to desired doneness.

✢ To serve, cut a 3-inch square of cornbread and place on each of 4 plates. Lean salmon fillets against cornbread and surround with blueberry barbecue sauce.

SERVES FOUR

Wild Alaskan Snapper with Stir-Fry Vegetable Curry and Quick Fried Noodles

Al Levinsohn, Kincaid Grill

Levinsohn learned some of his skills in Hong Kong and Thailand and thus some of his food has a bent toward fusion. This dish is a good example. Snapper, or rockfish, is a common catch. Although often overlooked because of the amount of salmon and halibut in the local fish store, Alaskan rockfish is clean-tasting and firm.

½ cup jasmine rice

3 tablespoons vegetable oil

4 Alaskan snapper fillets (6 ounces each) or other snapper

Salt and ground white pepper

1 to 2 tablespoons red curry paste, depending on heat desired

1 cup diced Japanese eggplant

4 lime leaves

1 cup julienned carrots

½ cup julienned red onion

⅓ cup julienned red bell pepper

⅓ cup julienned yellow bell pepper

⅓ cup julienned green bell pepper

¼ cup Fish Stock (page 197) or Chicken Stock (page 194)

¾ cup coconut milk

1 cup bean sprouts

½ cup julienned snow peas

½ cup julienned green onion

½ cup Thai basil, shredded

¼ cup cilantro, chopped

2 cups fried vermicelli or bean thread noodles

Cilantro leaves

✤ Place the jasmine rice in a dry sauté pan and toast over high heat, moving the rice constantly until it is a medium brown color. Remove from the pan immediately to prevent burning. Allow rice to cool. Place in a coffee grinder and pulse until coarsely ground. Set aside.

✤ Preheat the oven to 400°F.

✤ Heat 1 tablespoon of the vegetable oil in a 2-quart sauté pan over medium heat. Season the snapper fillets with salt and white pepper. Quickly sear the fillets on both sides to medium rare, dust generously on all sides with ground toasted rice, and place, skin side down, on a baking tray. Dissolve the curry paste in the remaining 2 tablespoons vegetable oil. Heat the mixture until hot, then add the eggplant, lime leaves, and carrots. Sauté for 1 minute. Add the red onion and bell peppers. Sauté until just heated through.

✤ Place fillets in the oven for 5 to 8 minutes, or until just done.

✤ While the fillets are in the oven, add the fish stock to the eggplant mixture and bring to a slow boil. Add the coconut milk and return to a boil. Add the bean sprouts, snow peas, green onion, basil, and cilantro, and remove from the heat.

✤ Divide the vegetable curry mixture among 4 warm plates. Top the curry with the fried noodles. Place the fillets on top of the noodles. Dust the plates with any remaining ground rice. Garnish with cilantro leaves and serve.

SERVES FOUR

Jerk-Dusted Kodiak Scallops with Citrus Beurre Blanc

Brett Knipmeyer, Kinley's

When buying your large sea scallops, be sure to ask for them "dry." Dry scallops are not processed with phosphates and are therefore a finer product for your table. Knipmeyer treats them simply here, with a hint of jerk seasoning to give them an exotic twist.

CITRUS BEURRE BLANC

½ cup freshly squeezed orange juice

¼ cup freshly squeezed lime juice

¼ cup freshly squeezed lemon juice

½ cup white wine

½ cup heavy cream

1 tablespoon minced shallot

1½ teaspoons jerk seasoning

1 teaspoon honey

½ cup (1 stick) unsalted butter, cut into pieces

½ teaspoon orange zest

½ teaspoon lime zest

½ teaspoon lemon zest

Salt and freshly ground black pepper

ACCOMPANIMENTS

1 cup jasmine rice

4 bunches baby bok choy, quartered

Salt and freshly ground black pepper

1 large green plantain

1 cup canola oil

JERK-DUSTED KODIAK SCALLOPS

16 Kodiak or other large sea scallops

1 tablespoon jerk seasoning

Salt and freshly ground black pepper

2 tablespoons canola oil

GARNISH

½ cup toasted unsweetened coconut flakes

⚜ To make the beurre blanc, simmer the orange juice, lime and lemon juices, white wine, cream, shallot, jerk seasoning, and honey until reduced by three-quarters (you should end up with just over ½ cup liquid). Remove from heat and whip in butter one piece at a time. Strain, stir in orange, lime, and lemon zests. Season with salt and pepper and reserve at room temperature (do not reheat).

⚜ To make the accompaniments, preheat a grill. Cook rice and keep warm. Blanch the bok choy for 1 minute in simmering water and drain. Mark on grill and season with salt and pepper. Reserve and keep warm. Cut the plantain in thin strips lengthwise, fry in canola oil until crisp, and drain on paper towels. Reserve and keep warm. Season with salt and pepper.

⚜ To make the scallops, dust scallops with jerk seasoning and season with salt and pepper. Heat the canola oil over medium-high heat until it shimmers, and sear scallops for about 1 minute on each side. Keep warm.

⚜ To serve, pool the beurre blanc on 4 warm plates, placing a mound of rice off-center on each. Lean bok choy and fried plantains against the rice. Place scallops in front and garnish with coconut flakes.

SERVES FOUR

Grilled Kodiak Scallops with Roasted Red Pepper Sauce

Jens Nannestad, Southside Bistro

This dish is good with Polenta Fritters (page 172). The trick is to cook the scallops only until they are rare or medium-rare.

ROASTED RED PEPPER SAUCE

4 Roma tomatoes, cored
6 cloves garlic, peeled
½ jalapeño pepper, chopped
½ small red onion, chopped
1 tablespoon olive oil
1 roasted red pepper, peeled and seeded
4 teaspoons aged balsamic vinegar
½ teaspoon salt
Pinch of freshly ground black pepper

SCALLOPS

1½ pounds Kodiak scallops or other large sea scallops
Salt and freshly ground black pepper
Polenta Fritters (page 172)

✢ Preheat the oven to 400°F.

✢ To make the sauce, combine the tomatoes, garlic, jalapeño, red onion, and olive oil in a heavy ovenproof pan. Roast in the oven until the tomato skin blackens and blisters, 45 to 60 minutes. Combine the tomato mixture with the red pepper, vinegar, salt, and pepper in a food processor. Process until smooth. Taste for salt and pepper.

✢ Preheat the grill.

✢ To prepare the scallops, season with salt and pepper. Grill until medium rare, about 1 minute on each side. Or use a sauté pan over high heat.

✢ Serve the scallops on a bed of roasted pepper sauce with the polenta fritters.

SERVES FOUR

Pepper-Crusted Sashimi Ahi with Cucumber Coulis and Wasabi Vinaigrette

Steve Gadbois, Sacks Cafe

The seared sashimi trend did not skip Alaska. Since Alaskans have a palate for fish and Asian flavors, it was sure to catch on. A hot sauté pan and excellent, best-quality tuna are key to this dish.

    1 cup roughly chopped peeled and seeded cucumber
    1 cup plain yogurt
    ½ teaspoon crushed red pepper
    1 teaspoon salt
    2 tablespoons wasabi powder
    2 tablespoons water
    ½ cup tamari
    2 tablespoons sesame oil
    1 pound sushi grade tuna
    2 tablespoons Szechuan peppercorns
    4 tablespoons vegetable oil
    3 heads of baby bok choy, roughly chopped
    ½ cup bean sprouts
    4 cups cooked jasmine rice
    Daikon sprouts, for garnish

✢ Place the cucumber, yogurt, red pepper, and salt in a food processor and process until smooth. Refrigerate.

✢ Combine the wasabi powder and water in a small bowl and mix to a paste. Blend in the tamari. Whisk in the sesame oil in a thin, steady stream. Taste to determine if salt is needed. Set aside.

✢ Trim the tuna, then portion it into 4 equal pieces. Grind the peppercorns until coarse and dust the outside of each piece of tuna with them. Add 2 tablespoons of the vegetable oil to a heavy skillet and place over medium-high heat until the oil shimmers. Sear each side of the tuna for 30 seconds. Keep warm.

✦ Add the remaining vegetable oil to the skillet and briefly sauté the bok choy and bean sprouts together. Add the rice and heat through.

✦ Divide the cucumber coulis equally among 4 plates. Place one fourth of the rice-vegetable mixture on top of the coulis. Top with tuna. Drizzle wasabi vinaigrette around the outside of the plate, sprinkle daikon sprouts on top for garnish, and serve.

SERVES FOUR

Halibut Baked in Macadamia Nuts with Coconut Curry and Mango Chutney

Jack Amon, The Marx Bros. Cafe

This Thai-influenced dish might be Amon's most famous recipe. He receives numerous requests for it. The fish is sturdy enough to stand up to the flavors of a variety of ingredients and takes well to the subtle Thai spicing.

RED CURRY PASTE

3 dried red Thai chiles

1 small onion, chopped

½ teaspoon freshly ground black pepper

1 teaspoon ground cumin

1½ teaspoons ground coriander

1 tablespoon chopped cilantro

½ teaspoon salt

1 tablespoon chopped lemongrass

1 clove garlic, chopped

1 teaspoon *kapi* (dried shrimp paste, available at Asian markets)

1 teaspoon vegetable oil

½ teaspoon turmeric

1 teaspoon paprika

HALIBUT

¾ cup flour

1 cup macadamia nuts

1½ pounds halibut fillet, skinned and cut into 4 equal portions

Salt and freshly ground black pepper

2 eggs, beaten with 2 tablespoons water

Vegetable oil spray

Pinch of cayenne

4 tablespoons (½ stick) butter, melted

PRESENTATION

2 tablespoons peanut oil

3 cups coconut milk

Mango Chutney (recipe follows)

✦ To make the red curry paste, remove the stems from the chiles but keep the seeds in if you want the paste to be as hot as it is in Thailand. Break the chiles into pieces; put in a blender or food processor together with the remaining curry paste ingredients. Blend to a smooth paste, stopping frequently to scrape down sides of bowl. It may be necessary to add a tablespoon of water or extra oil. Set aside.

✦ Preheat the oven to 375°F.

✦ To prepare the halibut, place the flour on a plate. Chop the nuts in a food processor, then with a knife by hand until there are no large pieces. Place on another large plate.

✦ About 15 minutes before serving, lightly season each fillet with salt and pepper. Dredge the fillets in the flour on both sides and shake off the excess. Dip both sides of the fillets in eggs, then directly into the nuts, pressing lightly. Lightly spray a baking sheet with vegetable oil spray or wipe lightly with vegetable oil. Place the fillets on the baking sheet so that they do not touch. Pour 1 tablespoon of melted butter on top of each fillet.

✦ Bake for 10 to 15 minutes, depending on the thickness of the fillets.

✦ While the halibut is cooking, finish the curry sauce. Heat the peanut oil in a heavy saucepan. Add ¼ cup red curry paste, reserving any left over for another use, and cook for 1 minute. Add the coconut milk and bring to a boil. Reduce by half. Keep warm.

✦ When the halibut is done, divide the curry sauce among 4 plates. Place the halibut on top of the sauce and garnish with a quarter of the mango chutney.

SERVES FOUR

Mango Chutney

¼ teaspoon minced dried Thai chiles

1 clove garlic

1 tablespoon peeled and minced fresh ginger

6 tablespoons rice vinegar

2 tablespoons sugar

1 large firm mango, peeled and diced

1 tablespoon chopped cilantro

⚓ Combine the chiles, garlic, and ginger in a blender or food processor with 1 tablespoon of the rice vinegar and process. Combine the chile mixture with the remaining vinegar and the sugar in small saucepan, bring to a boil, and reduce heat to a simmer for 5 minutes.

⚓ Remove from the heat, add the mango and cilantro, and allow chutney to cool before serving.

SERVES FOUR

Lemon-Pepper Halibut with Oven-Roasted Tomato-Basil Vinaigrette

Michele Camera-Faurot, Cafe Michele

Camera-Faurot created this recipe for a segment on the Food Network's "The Best Of: Places to Take Dad" to celebrate Father's Day for her employee's dad. Jill, her father, her brother, Michele, and a camera crew flew to a nearby glacier for the shooting. With remote cooking gear, food, wine, and flowers, the crew ate and filmed a heartfelt occasion.

OVEN-ROASTED TOMATO-BASIL VINAIGRETTE

3 Roma tomatoes, cut into 8 cubes per tomato

1 tablespoon plus ¾ cup olive oil

1 teaspoon minced garlic

2 tablespoons thinly sliced fresh basil

2 tablespoons minced sun-dried tomatoes

¼ cup raspberry vinegar

Salt and freshly ground black pepper

LEMON-PEPPER HALIBUT

1½-pound halibut fillet

2 tablespoons freshly ground black pepper

2 tablespoons ground lemon peel

1 teaspoon ground coriander

½ teaspoon onion powder

½ teaspoon sea salt

¼ cup Clarified Butter (page 203)

4 cups organic mesclun greens

✦ To make the vinaigrette, preheat the oven to 350°F. In a bowl, combine tomatoes, 1 tablespoon of the olive oil, and garlic. Place tomato mixture on a sheet pan lined with parchment paper (reserve bowl). Roast tomatoes for 15 minutes; return to the bowl. Add basil and sun-dried tomatoes and allow mixture to cool slightly. Add vinegar and remaining ¾ cup of olive oil. Season with salt and pepper.

✤ To make the halibut, cut fillet into 4 pieces. Combine pepper, lemon peel, coriander, onion powder, and salt. Sprinkle lemon-pepper mixture over the skin side of each fillet. Heat butter in large sauté pan over medium-high heat. When the butter begins to slowly bubble, add the fillets, skin side down. Cover pan and cook for 2 minutes. Uncover and continue cooking for another 3 minutes. Turn the fillets and cook on the other side until they are just done. Divide the mesclun greens among 4 plates, top with halibut (seasoned side up), and dress with vinaigrette.

SERVES FOUR

Tempura Halibut Cheeks with Caramelized Apple Gastrique and Candied Hop Polenta

Brett Knipmeyer, Kinley's

Traditionally, halibut cheeks—found logically in the heads—were awarded to the crew who landed the fish. If the fishermen had their fill, the cheeks would be, in turn, awarded to the crew on the docks. These nuggets of culinary delight are now available to thankful customers on land. A gastrique *is a classic French sauce that is a reduction of fruit, sugar, and vinegar. Hops may be found at your local brewers' supply, and while not absolutely necessary to make this recipe, they make a very interesting addition to Knipmeyer's polenta. Yellow cornmeal may be substituted for the polenta.*

CARAMELIZED APPLE GASTRIQUE

½ cup sliced yellow onion

2 Granny Smith apples, peeled, cored, and sliced

2 tablespoons butter

2 tablespoons sugar

3 tablespoons water

⅓ cup apple cider vinegar

⅓ cup Vegetable Stock (page 196)

Pinch of ground cinnamon

Pinch of ground nutmeg

Scant pinch of ground cloves

½ teaspoon cornstarch

CANDIED HOP POLENTA

2 tablespoons sugar

2 tablespoons water

⅓ cup loosely packed fresh hops

2 tablespoons butter

½ cup finely diced onion

1 cup polenta

3 cups Vegetable Stock (page 196)

¼ cup heavy cream

Salt and freshly ground black pepper

HALIBUT CHEEKS

      2 eggs

      2 cups sparkling water

      2½ cups flour

      Canola oil for frying

      1 pound halibut cheeks

      Salt and freshly ground black pepper

⚓ To make the *gastrique*, in a small saucepan cook the onion and apples in butter over medium-high heat until they are well browned (caramelized), about 13 minutes. In a large saucepan, add sugar to 2 tablespoons of the water and simmer for about 8 minutes, until sugar begins to caramelize. Allow mixture to cool slightly. Carefully add caramelized apple mixture (it will splatter!), vinegar, and vegetable stock. Mix well and return to a simmer. Add cinnamon, nutmeg, and cloves. Simmer for 10 minutes. Add cornstarch to remaining 1 tablespoon water to make a slurry. Stir the slurry into the *gastrique* and simmer for an additional 5 minutes. Reserve and keep warm.

⚓ To make the polenta, preheat the oven to 350°F. In a heavy saucepan, heat sugar and water to a gentle simmer. Swirl the pan occasionally, but do not stir. Remove the pan from the heat when the sugar water begins to caramelize, about 10 minutes. Place hops on a sheet pan and bake until just a little crispy, about 5 minutes; be careful not to burn. Stir the hops into the caramelized sugar and remove to a bowl to cool. When cool, chop hops and reserve. Melt butter in a large saucepan over medium heat, add onion, and sauté until the onion is soft but not brown, about 7 minutes. Add polenta, mixing well with the onion. Add vegetable stock, stirring constantly; bring to a simmer. Cook polenta, stirring often, for 10 minutes, or until soft. Add cream and candied hops; season with salt and pepper. Keep warm.

⚓ To make the halibut cheeks, whip eggs and stir in sparkling water. Whisk in flour (do not overmix) to make the tempura batter. Add enough canola oil in a deep skillet to cover cheeks; heat over high heat until oil registers 350°F on a deep-fat thermometer. Season cheeks with salt and pepper, dip in tempura, and deep-fry until just done, about 3 minutes. Drain on paper towels.

⚓ To serve, place a large spoonful of polenta on each of 4 warm plates. Divide halibut cheeks on top of the polenta and surround with *gastrique*.

    SERVES FOUR

Hazelnut-Crusted Halibut with Citrus-Thyme Cream

Elizabeth King, Southside Bistro

This is a great springtime recipe. It goes well with Fiddlehead and Wild Mushroom Relish (page 178).

CITRUS-THYME CREAM

> 1 orange, zest and juice
>
> 1 lemon, zest and juice
>
> 1 shallot, minced
>
> ½ cup dry white wine
>
> 1 teaspoon white peppercorns
>
> 1¼ cups heavy cream
>
> 2 teaspoons chopped fresh thyme
>
> 3 tablespoons butter, cut into 4 pieces
>
> Salt

HALIBUT

> ½ cup raw hazelnuts
>
> ½ cup panko (Japanese bread crumbs, available in Asian grocery stores and some supermarkets)
>
> 2 teaspoons Italian parsley leaves
>
> Salt and freshly ground black pepper
>
> 4 halibut fillets (6 ounces each)
>
> 1 egg, beaten
>
> Olive oil, for frying

✢ To make the citrus-thyme cream, combine the orange and lemon juices (reserve zests for later), shallot, wine, and peppercorns in a medium nonreactive saucepan over high heat. Bring to a low boil and reduce by two-thirds. Strain, then return to the saucepan. Add the cream and bring to a simmer over medium heat. Adjust the heat to maintain a bare simmer so that the cream does not scorch. Simmer until the sauce is reduced by one third.

✢ Remove from the heat and add the thyme. Whip in the butter, one piece at a time, until melted and well incorporated. Salt to taste. Fold in orange and lemon zests. Hold at room temperature; do not reheat.

✤ Preheat the oven to 400°F.

✤ To prepare the halibut, put the hazelnuts, panko, parsley, and a pinch of salt and pepper in a food processor. Process until most of the hazelnuts are very small, with just a few larger pieces.

✤ Season the fillets lightly with salt and pepper. Dip the presentation side of a fillet into the beaten egg, then press firmly into the nut mixture. Repeat with remaining fillets.

✤ In an overproof skillet large enough to hold all the fillets, pour enough olive oil to cover the bottom by ⅛ inch. Heat the oil over medium-high heat until it shimmers. Add the fillets, nut side down. Cook until the nuts get to be an even light golden brown. Gently turn the fillets over. Place the pan in the oven and roast until the fish is just cooked through; it should be very moist. Serve right away with the citrus-thyme cream.

SERVES FOUR

Herb-Crusted Halibut

Farrokh Larijani, Glacier BrewHouse

This dish is one of the workhorses at Glacier BrewHouse. During the summer, they sell more than a thousand orders a month.

CILANTRO OIL

½ cup olive oil

¼ cup cilantro

HALIBUT

4 halibut fillets, skin off (6 ounces each)

¾ teaspoon kosher salt

¼ teaspoon freshly ground black pepper

¼ cup Basil Pesto (recipe follows)

½ cup fresh bread crumbs

PRESENTATION

6 cups baby lettuce mix

1¼ cups Roasted Tomato Vinaigrette (page 186)

✣ To make the cilantro oil, purée the oil and cilantro in a blender. Set aside ¼ cup and reserve remaining cilantro oil to garnish Southwestern dishes or as a base for a salad dressing.

✣ Preheat the oven to 500°F.

✣ To prepare the halibut, season the underside of the fillets with salt and pepper. Turn over and top each fillet with 1 tablespoon of the basil pesto. Divide the bread crumbs among the fillets and press them down lightly onto the fish. Place fillets in a roasting pan large enough to hold them without crowding. Roast the fish until just done. (Chef Larijani suggests cooking fish until an instant-read thermometer registers 120°F.)

✣ Toss the lettuce with ¼ cup of the roasted tomato vinaigrette. Place the dressed lettuce on one side of the dinner plates and top with the fillet. Spoon the remainder of the vinaigrette on the other side of the plates. Drizzle each plate with 1 tablespoon of cilantro oil and serve.

SERVES FOUR

Basil Pesto

1 cup chopped basil

¼ cup grated Parmesan

1 tablespoon minced garlic

¼ cup walnuts, toasted

½ cup olive oil

1¼ teaspoons salt

¼ teaspoon freshly ground black pepper

⚜ Put the basil, Parmesan, garlic, and walnuts in a blender or food processor. With the motor running on medium speed, add the olive oil in a thin, steady stream. Season with the salt and pepper. Refrigerate leftover pesto for a later use.

MAKES 1¼ CUPS

Peppered Halibut with Ginger Butter

Al Levinsohn, Kincaid Grill

This dish also works well on a grill.

> 8 tablespoons (1 stick) butter
> 2 teaspoon minced fresh ginger
> 1 teaspoon plus 1 tablespoon coarsely cracked black pepper
> 1 teaspoon minced garlic
> Kosher salt
> 4 Alaskan halibut fillets (5 ounces each)
> 2 tablespoons olive oil

✦ Place the butter, ginger, 1 teaspoon of the pepper, and garlic in a food processor or mixer. Process or whip until all ingredients are incorporated. Season with salt. Hold at room temperature.

✦ Season each fillet with the remaining 1 tablespoon pepper, pressing the pepper firmly into the flesh of the fish. Season each fillet with salt.

✦ Add the olive oil to a large skillet and heat over medium-high heat until the oil shimmers. Pan-sear the halibut, skin side up, until the fish forms a golden crust. Turn the fish over and cook until it is firm to the touch and just cooked through.

✦ Place the fillets on warm plates and top each with an equal amount of the ginger butter.

SERVES FOUR

Cold Poached Salmon with Mint Mayonnaise

David and JoAnn Lesh, Gustavus Inn

Arrange poached salmon fillets on lettuce leaves on a fish platter. Decorate with baby garden vegetables and garnish with lemon wedges, edible flowers, and herb leaves. Leave a spot on the platter for a small ramekin of mint mayonnaise.

MINT MAYONNAISE

 1 egg
 2 tablespoons plus ¾ cup vegetable oil
 2 tablespoons vinegar
 15 fresh mint leaves, or more to taste
 ½ teaspoon salt

SALMON

 1 medium onion, thinly sliced
 1 carrot, thinly sliced
 1 stalk celery, thinly sliced
 10 black peppercorns, cracked
 6 parsley stems
 ½ cup dry white wine
 2 quarts cold water
 1 lemon, halved
 1½ pounds Alaskan salmon fillet, skin off

GARNISH

 Baby garden vegetables, such as carrots, radish roses, and snow peas
 Lemon wedges, edible flowers, parsley, and mint leaves

 ⚶ Place the egg, 2 tablespoons of the oil, vinegar, mint leaves, and salt in a blender and mix on high speed for 1 minute. Reduce the speed to slow, then add the remaining ¾ cup oil in a thin, steady stream. Taste and adjust the seasoning. Refrigerate. Leftovers may be kept for up to 4 days.

 ⚶ Combine the onion, carrot, celery, peppercorns, parsley stems, wine, and water in a medium roasting pan or rectangular cake pan. Place on top of the stove and bring to a boil. Reduce the heat to very low and squeeze the lemon into the water. Toss the lemon in. When the poaching liquid is steaming, add the salmon. (It is very important that the liquid is only steaming, not boiling or simmering. Poaching is a gentle process.) Allow the salmon to just cook through, about 10 minutes. Remove. Refrigerate until well chilled.

✢ Transfer the fish to a platter and decorate with baby garden vegetables, lemon wedges, edible flowers, herbs, and a small ramekin of mint mayonnaise.

SERVES FOUR

How to Fillet a Salmon

Whether you catch your own salmon or buy a whole, gutted fish at the store, you'll need to know how to fillet it. The key to clean fillets with little waste is the right knife. A fillet knife with a long, thin blade is best. It must be absolutely sharp or you will end up pulverizing the flesh.

Here's how to fillet:

✢ If your fish is already gutted, as it should be from the fishmonger, make sure you rinse it well to remove any remaining blood.

✢ Hold the salmon by the tail with one hand (a towel can sometimes help).

✢ If the head is still attached, saw it off just behind the gills.

✢ Start at the backbone and cut steadily along one side of the fish from tail to head, exposing the bone.

✢ Start at the tail again and, keeping the knife parallel with the fish, slice the meat from the ribs. You can slowly pull the fillet away from the ribs as you cut.

✢ Flip the fish over and repeat.

✢ At this point, you should be able to lift the fish by the backbone and slice it away from the meat.

✢ Cut off the tail, trim off the belly skin and any rough edges of the meat and you should have two beautiful fillets.

—Glenn Denkler

Roasted Salmon with Sauce Verde

Farrokh Larijani, Glacier BrewHouse

The pungent Sauce Verde gives the salmon a serious kick. It can also be used as a dip for vegetables or even be tossed with pasta.

SAUCE VERDE

> 2 anchovy fillets
> ⅓ cup capers
> 1½ tablespoons minced garlic
> 2 cups parsley
> 2 tablespoons fresh lemon juice
> ½ teaspoon freshly ground black pepper
> ¼ cup fresh basil
> 2 tablespoons fresh mint
> 1½ teaspoons fresh thyme
> ½ cup olive oil
> Vegetable Stock (page 196)

SALMON

> 4 Alaskan salmon fillets, skin on (6 ounces each)
> 1 teaspoon freshly ground black pepper
> ¼ teaspoon granulated garlic
> 3 tablespoons chopped tarragon
> 3 tablespoons thinly sliced shallots
> 1 leek, white part, julienned
> 8 thin slices fresh lemon
> Olive oil
> ½ cup Lemon Aïoli (page 191)

✦ To make the sauce verde, place the anchovies, capers, garlic, parsley, lemon juice, pepper, basil, mint, and thyme in a blender. With the blender running, pour in the olive oil in a thin, steady stream. Add enough vegetable stock to bring the paste to sauce consistency.

✦ Preheat the oven to 450°F.

✣ With a sharp knife, pull the skin back from each fillet. Season with pepper and garlic. Place the tarragon, shallots, leek, and lemon slices on top. Put the skin back over the tarragon mixture. Place the fillets on an ovenproof pan and coat the salmon skin with olive oil.

✣ Roast in the oven until just done. Put the fillets on hot plates and top with lemon aïoli. Drizzle each plate with ¼ cup of the sauce verde.

SERVES FOUR

Lime Chili King Salmon

Michele Camera-Faurot, Cafe Michele

While staying upcountry in Maui one winter on a property generously bordered by lime trees, Camera-Faurot created this recipe; when she is back hibernating in Talkeetna, it reminds her of those sunny, warm days. The dish can be served as a main course or as a garnish for a salad.

1½-pound skinless king salmon fillet
¼ cup sesame oil
2 tablespoons light olive oil (not extra-virgin)
Juice of 6 limes
¼ cup sliced green onion
1 tablespoon minced fresh ginger
1 tablespoon minced garlic
Large pinch of crushed red pepper

⚜ Cut the fillet into four equal portions. Combine the sesame oil, olive oil, lime juice, green onion, ginger, garlic, and red pepper to make a marinade. Reserve a quarter of the marinade. Place the fillets in a single layer in a baking dish. Pour remaining marinade over the salmon. Cover with plastic wrap and refrigerate for 30 minutes. Turn the salmon over, cover, and refrigerate for 30 minutes more. Remove salmon, reserving the marinade, and refrigerate salmon for another hour.

⚜ Heat a griddle or large sauté pan over medium heat. Add salmon to the griddle, skin side up. Cover and cook until the meat has cooked halfway up the side of the fillet. Turn the fillets over, cover, and cook until just done. To serve, drizzle salmon with the reserved marinade.

SERVES FOUR

Cornmeal-Crusted Sockeye Salmon with Peach Pico de Gallo

Brett Custer, The Homestead Restaurant

Custer has a way with taking the common and making it uncommon. The folks in Homer flock to see what he is up to next. Here, he converts a traditional pico de gallo by adding fresh peaches. Nectarines are an easy substitution. The garnish is a wonderful foil to the crisp cornmeal–crusted red salmon.

PEACH PICO DE GALLO

2 ripe peaches, pitted and chopped

5 ripe Roma tomatoes, finely diced

3 tablespoons finely diced red onion

2 teaspoons minced garlic

1 tablespoon rice vinegar

1 tablespoon olive oil

2 tablespoons chopped fresh cilantro

1½ teaspoons salt

½ teaspoon freshly ground black pepper

CORNMEAL-CRUSTED SOCKEYE SALMON

2-pound sockeye salmon fillet

Canola oil for pan frying

¾ cup yellow cornmeal

½ teaspoon powdered garlic

½ teaspoon freshly ground black pepper

¾ teaspoon salt

½ teaspoon dry parsley

½ teaspoon curry powder

½ teaspoon cayenne

✦ To make the pico de gallo, fold all ingredients together. Reserve.

✦ To make the salmon, preheat the oven to 350°F. Cut fillet into four equal portions. Add enough canola oil in a large skillet to come halfway up the thickest part of the salmon. Heat the oil over medium-high heat until it is shimmering, but not smoking hot. Mix cornmeal, garlic, pepper, salt, parsley, curry powder, and cayenne in a bowl with a whisk. Dredge fillets in the cornmeal mixture and add to skillet. Cook until golden, turn, and then place in oven. Cook for 5 minutes, or until just done. Drain on paper towels.

✦ To serve, divide the pico de gallo equally among 4 dinner plates. Top with salmon.

SERVES FOUR

Pepper-Crusted Salmon with King Crab–Infused Mashed Potatoes and Shellfish Stock

Jack Amon, The Marx Bros. Cafe

This sophisticated dish uses all parts of the king crab legs and pairs salmon with flavored mashed potatoes, a bistro-style trend just starting to get popular in Alaska.

SHELLFISH BUTTER

8 ounces lobster or crab shells

1 cup (2 sticks) unsalted butter

POTATOES

2 pounds king crab legs, in shell

1½ pounds Yukon Gold potatoes, peeled and sliced

3 tablespoons unsalted butter, at room temperature

⅓ cup heavy cream, warmed

Salt and ground white pepper

3 tablespoons finely chopped chives

SALMON

4 salmon fillets (6 ounces each)

¾ cup peppercorns, crushed

¼ cup Clarified Butter (page 203) or vegetable oil

2 cups Shellfish Stock (page 199)

2 leeks, white parts only, cut into thin strips and fried

✢ Preheat the oven to 400°F.

✢ To prepare the shellfish butter, roast the shells until crisp and dry. Crush the shells with a hammer or food processor. Place the shells and butter in a heavy medium saucepan over low heat. When the butter is melted, continue to cook over low heat for 45 minutes. Skim the foam. Strain the butter, discarding the shells, and refrigerate.

✢ Shell the crab legs. Dice the meat and set aside. Set aside the shells.

✦ To prepare the potatoes, place them in a large, heavy pot and cover with salted water. Bring to a boil, then reduce to a simmer. Cook until the potatoes are soft. Drain. Transfer the potatoes to a mixing bowl and beat in 3 tablespoons of the shellfish butter, the unsalted butter, and the cream. Season with salt and pepper. Stir in the chives and reserved crabmeat. Keep warm.

✦ To prepare the salmon, lightly coat the presentation side of the fillets with the crushed pepper. Heat the clarified butter in a heavy ovenproof skillet over medium-high heat until very hot. Place the salmon fillets in the skillet, pepper side down, and cook for 5 to 7 minutes. Place the skillet in the oven, without turning the fish over, and cook for 7 to 10 minutes more, or until the salmon is just done.

✦ Divide the potatoes among 4 large pasta bowls. Place a salmon fillet, pepper side up, on top of the potatoes. Ladle shellfish stock over each portion, garnish with fried leeks, and serve.

SERVES FOUR

Halibut with Pistou in Parchment

Laura Cole, 229 Parks Restaurant and Tavern

This dish may be prepared with a variety of fish and a variety of cuts. A firm-fleshed, not too fatty fish is definitely preferred. For a party or large dinner gathering, it is very impressive to serve this as a whole fish with head and tail still attached and fillet it at the table.

PISTOU

> 4 large fresh garlic scapes or 4 large cloves garlic
>
> 1 teaspoon sea salt
>
> 2 cups loosely packed basil leaves
>
> ½ cup extra-virgin olive oil

HALIBUT

> 4 sprigs of thyme
>
> 4 fresh (or 3 dried) bay leaves
>
> 4 halibut fillets, approximately 1½ inches thick
>
> Sea salt and freshly ground pepper
>
> 2 medium organic tomatoes, peeled, seeded, and chopped
>
> 3 tablespoons extra-virgin olive oil
>
> 2 tablespoons fresh lemon juice

⚜ To make the pistou, using either a mortar and pestle or a food processor, purée the garlic, salt and basil. Add the olive oil slowly until the mixture is well blended. Leftover pistou may be refrigerated for 1 week or frozen.

⚜ To make the halibut, preheat the oven to 425°F. Cut a sheet of parchment paper large enough to comfortably enclose one halibut fillet. Place one sprig of thyme and one bay leaf on one side of the parchment paper. Place a fillet on top of the herbs. Season with salt and pepper. Top with 1 tablespoon of the pistou. Fold the parchment paper over the fillet and crimp the paper until it is sealed airtight (use a clip or staples if necessary). Repeat with the other three fillets. Transfer wrapped fillets to a baking tray and roast for 20 minutes. As the fish is roasting, slightly warm the tomatoes in the olive oil and 2 tablespoons of the pistou. Add lemon juice and season with salt and pepper. Remove the fillets from the oven. Being mindful of escaping steam, cut the packages open and let the fish rest for a minute. Transfer fish to warm plates and top with warmed tomato garnish.

SERVES FOUR

Almond-Crusted Halibut with Cider-Cherry Beurre Blanc

Brett Knipmeyer, Kinley's

Fresh cider from a spigot in an orchard would be perfect for Knipmeyer's signature dish. Organic cider is not as romantic, but it would certainly fit the bill.

CIDER-CHERRY BEURRE BLANC

1½ cups fresh or organic apple cider

1½ cups juice from canned dark sweet cherries

½ cup white wine

1 tablespoon minced shallot

½ cup heavy cream

½ cup (1 stick) unsalted butter, cut into pieces

16 dark sweet cherries

Sea salt

ALMOND-CRUSTED HALIBUT

4 halibut fillets (6 ounces each)

Sea salt and freshly ground black pepper

1 egg

1 cup milk

½ cup water

⅔ cup panko (Japanese bread crumbs, available in Asian markets and some supermarkets)

⅔ cup sliced almonds, lightly toasted

1 cup all-purpose flour

Canola oil

⁜ To make the beurre blanc, in a large saucepan simmer the cider, cherry juice, wine, shallot, and cream until reduced to just over ½ cup. Strain into another saucepan. Off heat, whip in the butter piece by piece until just melted. Add cherries. Season with salt. Keep warm, but do not reheat.

⁜ To make the halibut, season fillets with salt and pepper. Combine egg, milk, and water. In a food processor, pulse panko and almonds until mixture is the consistency of coarse meal. Dredge fillets in flour, dip in egg wash, then press into panko-almond mixture; reserve.

✛ In a large skillet, add enough canola oil to come halfway up the thickest part of the fillet; heat oil over medium-high heat until it shimmers. Add fillets in single layer, cook until golden; flip, cook until other side is golden and just done, about 6 minutes total. Drain on paper towels. Keep warm.

✛ To serve, divide beurre blanc among 4 warm plates. Top with halibut and garnish each fillet with 4 cherries from the sauce.

SERVES FOUR

Panko-Crusted Halibut with Roasted Tomato and Caper Relish

Brett Custer, The Homestead Restaurant

This flavorful relish would be a superb complement to any grilled or pan-fried seafood dish. It has just enough oomph without overpowering the main attraction.

ROASTED TOMATOES

12 Roma tomatoes

½ cup brown sugar

3 tablespoons salt

1 tablespoon freshly ground black pepper

¼ cup canola oil

ROASTED TOMATO AND CAPER RELISH

1 cup roughly chopped roasted tomatoes

¼ cup finely diced roasted red peppers

1 tablespoon capers

1 tablespoon extra-virgin olive oil

1½ teaspoons white vinegar

1 teaspoon chopped fresh oregano

1 tablespoon chopped fresh basil

Salt and freshly ground black pepper

PANKO-CRUSTED HALIBUT

Canola oil for frying

4 fresh halibut fillets (6 ounces each)

Salt and freshly ground black pepper

Panko for coating (Japanese bread crumbs, available in Asian markets and some supermarkets)

⚜ To make the roasted tomatoes, preheat the oven to 350°F. Core tomatoes and cut in half through the widest point. Toss tomato halves, brown sugar, salt, pepper, and canola oil in a bowl until well blended. Place tomato mixture on a sheet pan with the tomatoes cut side up. Bake for 1½ to 2 hours, or until beginning to brown and slightly dry. Allow mixture to cool. Refrigerate. Leave oven on for halibut.

✦ To make the relish, combine all ingredients well. Refrigerate for a minimum of 2 hours.

✦ To make the halibut, add enough canola oil in a sauté pan to come halfway up the side of the fillets. Over medium heat, heat oil until it shimmers. Season fillets with salt and pepper and dredge in panko, pressing lightly. Add fillets to oil, cook until golden, turn, and cook until other side is golden. Remove fillets to an oven-proof tray and cook in the oven for approximately 4 to 5 minutes, or until just done. Place briefly on paper towels to drain any excess oil.

✦ To serve, divide the relish among 4 warm plates, top with halibut fillets.

SERVES FOUR

Roasted Dungeness Crab with Pasta

Farrokh Larijani, Glacier BrewHouse

This dish is done in the wood-fired oven at the Glacier BrewHouse. You can get a similar effect in your home oven.

3 teaspoons kosher salt
4 pounds Dungeness crab legs, scored
¼ cup chopped parsley
¼ cup chopped basil
3 tablespoons minced garlic
1 cup olive oil
1 tablespoon black pepper, cracked
Juice of 2 lemons
12 ounces dried pasta, such as linguine or spaghetti
4 lemon wedges
8 sprigs of Italian parsley

✦ Preheat the oven to 400°F.

✦ Bring 3 quarts of water to a boil in a large stockpot with 2 teaspoons of the salt.

✦ Combine the crab, parsley, basil, garlic, olive oil, pepper, the remaining teaspoon salt, and lemon juice in a large bowl. Toss well. Place the crab legs in a roasting pan and drizzle with mixture left in the bowl.

✦ Roast the crab until it is almost heated through, about 8 minutes. Watching closely, finish the crab under the broiler until the edges just start to char.

✦ While the crab is roasting, cook the pasta until al dente. Drain.

✦ Divide the pasta among 4 plates. Arrange the crab legs around the pasta and drizzle crab and pasta with the remaining oil mixture from the roasting pan. Garnish each plate with a lemon wedge and 2 sprigs of parsley and serve.

SERVES FOUR

Grilled Wild Alaskan Salmon with Tomato-Arugula Salsa

Jens Nannestad, Southside Bistro

The secret of preparing great seafood is to not overcook it. The preferred salmon for this recipe would be the first run of the famous Copper River King salmon. However, any fresh salmon or other fresh broiler–friendly fish will certainly suit this recipe.

TOMATO-ARUGULA SALSA

8 Roma tomatoes, cored and diced small

¾ cup chopped arugula

1 shallot, finely chopped

2 cloves garlic, minced

2 tablespoons capers

3 tablespoons fresh lemon juice

¾ teaspoon salt

¼ teaspoon freshly ground black pepper

1½ tablespoons olive oil

SALMON

1¾ pounds salmon fillet

½ cup Herb Olive Oil (recipe follows)

Kosher salt and freshly ground black pepper

⚜ To make the salsa, combine all the ingredients and refrigerate.

⚜ Preheat the grill.

⚜ To prepare the salmon, skin, trim, and remove the pin bones from the salmon fillet. Divide into 4 equal portions. Brush the fish with the herb olive oil and season lightly with salt and pepper.

⚜ Grill on a very hot grill until just done. Baste with more herb olive oil during the cooking.

⚜ When done, place each piece of fish on a warm plate, top with one fourth of the salsa, and serve.

SERVES FOUR

Herb Olive Oil

⅓ cup olive oil

2 tablespoons basil

2 tablespoons parsley

2 teaspoons marjoram

1 teaspoon thyme

✦ Purée the oil and herbs in a blender.

MAKES ½ CUP

Grilled Salmon with Balsamic Reduction and Tomato-Leek Relish

JoAnn Asher, Sacks Cafe

The reduction of vinegar adds a sharp-sweet note to the rich salmon. The smoky relish is a perfect foil.

TOMATO-LEEK RELISH

6 Roma tomatoes

1 leek, white part only, halved, sliced, and cleaned

2 teaspoons chopped garlic

1 teaspoon salt

1 teaspoon granulated sugar

2 tablespoons olive oil

SALMON

1½ pounds salmon fillet

24 ounces balsamic vinegar

3 tablespoons (packed) brown sugar

1 tablespoon Worcestershire sauce

½ teaspoon crushed red pepper

✢ Preheat the oven to 350°F.

✢ To make the relish, core and quarter the tomatoes. Add the leek, garlic, salt, sugar, and olive oil. Gently mix until combined. Place the tomato mixture in a baking pan or Pyrex dish. Roast for 20 minutes, or until the tomato skins start to wrinkle. Keep warm.

✢ To prepare the salmon, skin and trim the fillet, cut into 4 equal portions, and set aside.

✢ In a small saucepan, reduce the balsamic vinegar by two-thirds, about 30 minutes.

✢ Preheat the grill.

✢ Add brown sugar, Worcestershire sauce and red pepper. Simmer 3 to 5 minutes, or until of syrup-like consistency. Remove from the heat and let rest 5 minutes before use. (This reduction keeps very well in the refrigerator. Bring it to room temperature before using.)

✢ Grill the salmon for 5 to 10 minutes, or until just done. Place on a warm plate, drizzle with the balsamic reduction, and top with the relish.

SERVES FOUR

A Salmon Primer

To many cooks, Alaska is synonymous with salmon, and with good reason. Each year, nearly 200 million wild salmon are commercially harvested in Alaska. Hundreds of thousands more are taken by sport anglers or by Alaska Natives who use the fish to sustain them through the winter. Although five different species are harvested, three show up regularly in restaurants and in home kitchens: kings (chinooks), silvers (cohos), and reds (sockeyes).

Silvers are known as fine fighting fish. Reds are one of Alaska's favorite eating fish, and kings, also prized, are the largest. A 120-pound king salmon is thought to have spent about seven years in the ocean.

The superior flavor and firm, meaty flesh of wild salmon are worth searching for. Farm-raised salmon, often from the Atlantic Ocean, are pale and mushy in comparison. Wild Alaskan salmon can sometimes be found at fish markets in the Lower 48, and Alaskan fish companies will ship fresh salmon (see page 234). If you live on the West Coast, wild king salmon from the Pacific Northwest or the California coast is seasonally available and a reasonable alternative.

—Kim Severson

Sesame-Crusted Salmon with Miso Vinaigrette

Jack Amon, The Marx Bros. Cafe

The crunch of the sesame seeds and the bright flavors of the miso sauce make for a stunning combination.

MISO VINAIGRETTE

2½ tablespoons white miso

2 tablespoons fresh lemon juice

1 tablespoon Thai sweet chile sauce

2 tablespoons rice wine vinegar

1½ teaspoons finely chopped garlic

1½ teaspoons finely chopped shallot

3 tablespoons peeled and finely chopped fresh ginger

2 tablespoons soy sauce

1 tablespoon dry sherry or mirin

1 teaspoon sugar

1 cup peanut oil

¼ cup sesame oil

3 green onions, sliced very thin

SALMON

1½ pounds salmon fillet

⅓ cup white sesame seeds

⅓ cup black sesame seeds

¼ cup vegetable oil

4 heads of baby bok choy, steamed

6 ounces ogo or other seaweed (available at Asian markets and some seafood stores), steamed

✤ To make the miso vinaigrette, put all the ingredients except the peanut and sesame oils and the green onions into a food processor and process until smooth. With the motor running, slowly add the oils. Remove the vinaigrette to a bowl, add the green onions, and set aside.

✤ Preheat the oven to 400°F.

✤ Skin, trim, and debone salmon, if not already done. Cut into 4 equal fillets.

✤ In a bowl, combine the white and black sesame seeds. Press the presentation side of each fillet into the seeds.

✤ Heat the vegetable oil in a heavy ovenproof skillet until it shimmers. Sear the sesame-crusted side of the salmon about 3 minutes or until the white seeds are golden. Turn the fillets to other side. Transfer the pan to the oven and cook for about 10 minutes, or until just done. Drain on paper towels.

✤ Transfer the salmon to 4 warmed plates, top each with ¼ cup of vinaigrette, reserving any leftover vinaigrette for another use. Garnish with the steamed bok choy and seaweed and serve.

SERVES FOUR

Sesame Salmon Cakes with Soy-Ginger Glaze

Elizabeth King, Southside Bistro

The pronounced flavor of wild salmon is preferred for this recipe, but farmed Atlantic salmon will do in a pinch.

SALMON CAKES

20 ounces raw Alaskan salmon
⅓ cup minced red onion
⅓ cup minced celery
¾ cup minced red bell pepper
2 green onions, thinly sliced
½ jalapeño, minced
¼ cup finely chopped cilantro
3 teaspoons sesame oil
1¾ teaspoons kosher salt
Freshly ground black pepper
3 tablespoons soy sauce
3 tablespoons heavy cream
2 tablespoons flour
1 egg white
1 tablespoon fresh lemon juice
Vegetable oil
¼ cup black sesame seeds
¼ cup white sesame seeds
¼ cup flour

SOY-GINGER GLAZE

¾ cup soy sauce
6 tablespoons rice wine vinegar
10 tablespoons (packed) brown sugar
1 tablespoon chopped fresh ginger
1 tablespoon cornstarch
1 tablespoon cold water

✦ Divide the salmon into 2 portions, one weighing 12 ounces, the other 8 ounces. Finely chop the 12-ounce portion. Roughly chop the 8-ounce portion. Keep separate.

✦ Combine the 12-ounce portion of finely chopped salmon, red onion, celery, bell pepper, green onions, jalapeño, cilantro, 1½ teaspoons of the sesame oil, 1 teaspoon of the salt, and ¼ teaspoon of pepper in a mixing bowl. Cover and refrigerate until chilled.

✦ Put the 8-ounce portion of roughly chopped salmon, the soy sauce, cream, flour, egg white, lemon juice, the remaining 1½ teaspoons of sesame oil, the remaining ¾ teaspoon salt, and a pinch of pepper in a food processor. Purée until smooth, scraping down the sides of the bowl during the process. Remove to a large bowl.

✦ Fold in the finely chopped salmon mixture. Make a small patty, pan-fry in a small amount of oil. Taste for seasoning. Adjust with more salt and/or pepper to taste. Make another test patty if necessary. Shape into 8 patties for a main course or 16 for appetizers. Cover and refrigerate for 4 hours.

✦ Meanwhile, mix together the black and white sesame seeds and flour. Set aside.

✦ Shortly before serving, prepare the soy-ginger glaze. Combine the soy sauce, vinegar, brown sugar, and ginger in a small saucepan. Bring to a simmer. Mix the cornstarch and water in a teacup until well combined. Whisk the cornstarch mixture into the soy sauce mixture. Simmer 5 minutes, then strain.

✦ To serve, dredge the patties in the sesame-seed mixture. Pan-fry in vegetable oil on each side until golden, about 4 to 5 minutes. Drain on paper towels and serve with the soy-ginger glaze. Discard any remaining sesame seed mixture.

SERVES FOUR AS A MAIN COURSE OR EIGHT AS AN APPETIZER

Scallops in Saffron and Pernod Cream Sauce with Caviar

Jens Hansen, Jens' Restaurant

Anise liqueur and saffron are a classic flavor combination. The sauce is delicate enough not to overpower the scallops. The caviar gives the dish an elegant touch.

24 sea scallops
2 tablespoons Clarified Butter (page 203)
2 ounces Pernod
1 cup Fish Stock (page 197) or clam juice
¼ teaspoon saffron threads
1 cup heavy cream
2 tablespoons butter
2 ounces beluga or other caviar

⚓ Pan-fry the scallops in clarified butter in a smoking hot pan for 20 seconds on each side. Remove the scallops and keep warm; don't clean out the frying pan.

⚓ Add the Pernod, fish stock, and saffron. Reduce the liquid to 6 tablespoons over high heat. Stir in the heavy cream and reduce to ½ cup. Remove the pan from the heat and whip in the butter.

⚓ Divide the sauce among 4 plates. Place the scallops on the sauce and sprinkle caviar over the shellfish. Serve right away.

SERVES FOUR

Sesame-Crusted Weathervane Scallops with Wild Mushrooms and Tomatillo Salsa

Brett Custer, The Homestead Restaurant

Weathervane scallops, found in the waters near Kodiak, are one of the sweetest culinary treats on earth. But any large scallop works well in this dish. Be sure to ask your purveyor for "dry," not "wet" scallops: wet scallops are soaked in water containing phosphates. Some of this water is absorbed (you are paying a high price for water) and interferes with proper browning when the scallops are sautéed. Dry scallops are wild, natural, and without any additives.

TOMATILLO SALSA

12 ounces tomatillos, husked and halved
4 cloves garlic, chopped
1 cup chopped white onion
½ cup chopped cilantro
Salt and freshly ground black pepper

WILD MUSHROOMS

1 tablespoon canola oil
1 tablespoon minced shallot
½ pound mixed wild mushrooms, cleaned and roughly chopped
1 teaspoon minced garlic
¼ cup dry white wine
1 tablespoon butter
Salt and freshly ground black pepper

SESAME-CRUSTED WEATHERVANE SCALLOPS

2 tablespoons canola oil
1 pound weathervane or other large sea scallops
Salt and freshly ground black pepper
¼ cup sesame seeds

✧ To make the tomatillo salsa, bring enough water to cover tomatillos to a boil. Lower heat, add tomatillos, garlic, and onion, and simmer for 5 minutes. Drain and reserve water. In a food processor, purée tomatillo mixture briefly until it achieves a coarse consistency, adding just enough reserved water to make the salsa smooth. Stir in cilantro, season with salt and pepper, and keep warm.

✦ To prepare the wild mushrooms, heat the canola oil in a sauté pan over medium-high heat until it shimmers. Add shallot and mushrooms. Cook, stirring, for 5 minutes; add garlic, cook for 1 minute more. Add white wine and cook until most of the moisture evaporates; remove from heat. Fold in butter, stir until it melts. Season with salt and pepper and keep warm.

✦ To prepare the scallops, heat the canola oil in sauté pan over medium-high heat until it shimmers. Season the scallops with salt and pepper, then press the sesame seeds into the scallops on each side. Sear the scallops on both sides, about 2 minutes on each side.

✦ To serve, divide the salsa among 4 warm plates. Place the scallops on top of the salsa. Arrange the wild mushrooms over and among the scallops.

SERVES FOUR

Alaskan Spot Shrimp and Smoked Gouda Polenta Tart with Avocado Salsa

Toby Ramey, Sacks Cafe

Alaskan spot shrimp are sweet and plump, and are sometimes sold with a pocket of orange roe in their bellies. Tiger or other shrimp can be substituted.

AVOCADO SALSA

4 Roma tomatoes, cored and diced

½ red onion, finely diced

1 jalapeño, finely diced, seeded if you like it mild

2 avocados, diced

Juice of ½ lime

1½ teaspoons minced garlic

¼ cup chopped cilantro

Salt and freshly ground black pepper

TART

2 teaspoons olive oil

½ teaspoon ground cumin

½ teaspoon granulated garlic

½ teaspoon ancho chile powder

½ teaspoon dried thyme

1½ pounds Alaskan spot shrimp or tiger shrimp (26–30 per pound), peeled and deveined

2¼ cups water

2 tablespoons butter

1 teaspoon kosher salt

½ cup polenta

½ cup yellow cornmeal

½ cup grated smoked gouda

Nonstick vegetable oil spray

✦ To make the avocado salsa, mix together the tomatoes, onion, jalapeño, avocados, lime juice, garlic, and cilantro and season with salt and pepper. Set aside.

✦ Preheat the oven to 325°F.

✤ To make the tart, combine the olive oil, cumin, garlic, chile powder, and thyme in a large bowl. Add the shrimp and toss to coat. Refrigerate.

✤ Combine the water, butter, and salt in a large saucepan and bring to a boil. Mix together the polenta and cornmeal and add the mixture to the boiling water. Whisk until smooth with no lumps. Over low heat, stir the polenta with a wooden spoon for 3 minutes. Remove from the heat. Add gouda and stir until melted. The polenta should be thick, but spreadable.

✤ Spray a 9-inch tart pan (with a removable bottom) with nonstick spray. Arrange the shrimp evenly around the bottom of the tart pan, leaving a ½-inch border. Starting at the outside of the tart pan, use a rubber spatula to fill the border between the pan and the shrimp with the polenta mixture. Spread the remaining polenta mixture over the shrimp and smooth it to a uniform thickness. Bake for 10 minutes, or until polenta is firm, not crisp. Invert onto a cutting board and cut into 6 wedges.

✤ Place on warm plates, garnish with salsa, and serve.

SERVES SIX

Ricotta Cavatelli with Alaskan Side Stripe Shrimp

Michele Camera-Faurot, Cafe Michele

Cavatelli is similar to gnocchi, but without the potato. It is worth the time and effort to make this culinary treat: you will never go back to gnocchi again. Camera-Faurot was introduced to cavatelli while she was working in a local Italian restaurant during her high school years. Fresh imported ricotta (or homemade) is essential for making this tender pasta. Side stripe shrimp is a cold-water shellfish similar to spot shrimp. These delicate crustaceans are prized by all Alaskan cooks.

RICOTTA CAVATELLI

8 ounces fresh whole-milk Italian ricotta cheese

¾ to 1 cup unbleached flour, plus extra for kneading

⅓ cup grated Romano cheese

1 large organic egg

Pinch of salt

ALASKAN SIDE STRIPE SHRIMP

⅓ cup olive oil

1½ pounds fresh Alaskan side stripe shrimp (26–30 per pound), peeled and deveined

1 teaspoon minced garlic

Salt and freshly ground black pepper

½ cup grated Romano cheese

1 tablespoon lemon zest

½ cup thinly sliced fresh basil

⚜ To make the cavatelli, mix the ricotta, flour, Romano, egg, and salt in a stand mixer fitted with a dough hook attachment until a sticky dough is formed. (Feel free to do this by hand to be more traditional.) Turn the dough out on a well-floured board and knead lightly until it can be handled easily, adding more flour if necessary. Roll dough into a long log approximately 1 inch in diameter and cut the log into 2-inch pieces. Roll each piece in flour and let rest.

⚜ Take one piece at a time and, on a floured surface, roll out to resemble a snake a little less than ½ inch in diameter. Cut dough into 1-inch pieces. Roll in flour. Repeat with remaining dough.

✢ With your index and middle finger, press down into the dough pieces, then roll toward you to form a piece of pasta in the shape of a Parker House roll (flattened into an oval and then folded in half). Using about 1 cup of pasta per person (leftover pasta may be stored in an airtight container in the refrigerator for up to three days after being dusted generously with flour), add cavatelli to boiling salted water one cup at a time and cook until they float to the surface. Drain.

✢ To prepare the shrimp, heat the olive oil in a large sauté pan over medium-high heat until it shimmers. Add shrimp and stir well. Cook for 2 minutes. Add garlic, toss, and continue to cook until the shrimp are just done, about 2 minutes. Toss the shrimp with the cavatelli and season with salt and pepper. Divide among 4 warm bowls. Top with Romano, lemon zest, and basil.

SERVES FOUR

Sablefish Indochine

Brett Custer, The Homestead Restaurant

Sablefish is also known as black cod, although it is not in the cod family. It is found from Oregon and Washington all the way to the Aleutian Islands. Rich in omega-3 fatty acids, this delightful fish is gaining in popularity among chefs and is finally finding its way into the home. Traditionally smoked, sablefish lends itself to a large variety of cooking methods, including sautéing, poaching, grilling, and roasting. It has a mild and delicate flavor that is compatible with a variety of sauces and garnishes. Here is Custer's treatment.

SOY DEGLAZE

1 cup soy sauce

⅓ cup sesame oil

2 tablespoons hoisin sauce

1 teaspoon crushed red pepper

1 tablespoon minced garlic

1 tablespoon minced fresh ginger

ASIAN VEGETABLES

¼ cup sesame oil

1 cup julienned carrots

1 cup julienned red peppers

2 cups sliced oyster mushrooms

2 cups roughly chopped napa cabbage

1 teaspoon minced garlic

1 teaspoon minced fresh ginger

SABLEFISH

1 tablespoon sesame oil

2 tablespoons canola oil

4 sablefish fillets (6 ounces each)

Salt and freshly ground black pepper

Rice flour

GARNISH

> 4 ounces rice noodles, cooked according to package directions, drained,
> and kept warm
>
> ½ cup Mae Ploy sweet chili sauce
>
> ½ bunch cilantro, chopped

✤ To make the soy deglaze, combine all the ingredients, mix well, and reserve.

✤ To prepare the Asian vegetables, heat the sesame oil in a deep pan over high heat until it shimmers. Add carrots, red peppers, and mushrooms and stir-fry for 2 minutes. Add cabbage and ¼ cup of the soy deglaze, stir, and cover for 1 minute. Remove lid, stir in garlic and ginger. Cook, stirring, for 15 seconds; remove from heat, keep warm.

✤ To prepare the sablefish, preheat the oven to 350°F. Heat the sesame and canola oils in an ovenproof sauté pan over medium-high heat until they shimmer. Season the sablefish with salt and pepper, dredge in rice flour, and pan-fry the fish on both sides until golden. Place the pan in the oven to continue cooking fish for 3 to 5 minutes, or until just done. Drain fish on paper towels.

✤ To make the garnish, toss the rice noodles, Asian vegetables, chili sauce, and cilantro in a large bowl.

✤ To serve, divide garnish among 4 warm plates. Top with sablefish.

SERVES FOUR

Pan-Seared Sablefish with Wasabi Beurre Blanc and Sweet Soy Glaze

Brett Knipmeyer and Jim Nyholm, Kinley's

Also known as black cod, sablefish is prized for its sweet flesh. It is similar in texture to Chilean sea bass but is a far more environmentally superior dining choice. Be sure to remove the large pinbones with a pair of needle-nose pliers. Another plus for this fish is that it contains as many omega-3 fats as wild salmon.

WASABI BEURRE BLANC

2 tablespoons wasabi paste, or ¼ cup wasabi powder mixed with 3 tablespoons white wine

3 tablespoons white wine

½ cup soy sauce

2 teaspoons freshly cracked black pepper

10 tablespoons (1¼ sticks) unsalted butter, cut into 16 pieces

Honey

SWEET SOY GLAZE

1 teaspoon cornstarch

2 teaspoons mirin

⅔ cup soy sauce

1 tablespoon sugar

PAN-SEARED SABLEFISH

4 sablefish fillets (6 ounces each)

Salt and freshly ground black pepper

1 teaspoon sesame oil

1 tablespoon canola oil

VEGETABLE SAUTÉ

4 ounces rice stick noodles

1½ cups sugar snap peas

1 red bell pepper, julienned

1 teaspoon sesame oil

1 tablespoon canola oil

1 teaspoon shaved fresh ginger

1 teaspoon minced garlic

      1 tablespoon toasted black sesame seeds

      1 green onion, sliced thinly on the bias

⚶ To make the beurre blanc, mix wasabi paste and wine together to form a slurry. In a small saucepan, bring wasabi slurry, soy sauce, and pepper to a simmer. Remove from heat and whisk in the butter a few pieces at a time. Add honey to taste. Hold at room temperature.

⚶ To make the soy glaze, make a slurry of the cornstarch and mirin. In a small saucepan, heat the soy sauce and sugar to a simmer. Whip in slurry and simmer until glaze is reduced by a third; reserve.

⚶ To prepare the sablefish, preheat the oven to 300°F. Season the fish lightly with salt and pepper. Over high heat, pan-sear the fillets in the sesame and canola oils on both sides until golden. Remove the fish to a baking tray and place in the oven to finish cooking until just done.

⚶ To make the vegetable sauté, soak the noodles in warm water to soften; drain and reserve. Blanch sugar snap peas in simmering water for 1 minute, drain, shock in ice water, drain again. Sauté red pepper for 1 minute in the sesame and canola oils. Add sugar snap peas, ginger, and garlic and sauté for 30 seconds. Add noodles and toss until heated through.

⚶ To serve, divide vegetable sauté among 4 warm plates and top each plate with a sablefish fillet. Spoon beurre blanc around the fillet in a circle. Drizzle fish with glaze. Garnish with sesame seeds and green onion.

SERVES FOUR

Blue-Cornmeal-Crusted Alaskan Oysters with Smoked Corn and Horseradish Cream Sauce

Brett Knipmeyer, Kinley's

When fresh corn is in season, you can bet that Alaska's year–round fresh oysters are there to be enjoyed with them. The lightly smoked corn flavor marries well with the cornmeal crust surrounding the plump oysters.

SMOKED CORN AND HORSERADISH CREAM SAUCE

1 cup hardwood chips (such as hickory, cherry, or apple) soaked for 1 hour

2 ears corn, husked and silk removed

½ cup diced yellow onion

½ cup diced red pepper

1 tablespoon canola oil

2 teaspoons minced garlic

1 teaspoon grated horseradish

1 cup heavy cream

Salt and freshly ground black pepper

BLUE-CORNMEAL-CRUSTED ALASKAN OYSTERS

24 fresh Alaskan oysters

Canola oil for frying

Salt and freshly ground black pepper

2 cups blue cornmeal

GARNISH

¼ cup sliced green onions

¼ cup finely diced red pepper

⚜ To make the corn and cream sauce, preheat one burner on a gas grill or heat one quart of coals on one side of a charcoal grill. Place hardwood chips on an 8-inch piece of heavy-duty aluminum foil. Fold the edges of the foil into a makeshift tray. Place on the grill over the hot spot and cover grill. After 15 minutes, place the corn on the cooler side of the grill. Cover and cook the corn for 10 minutes. Reserve corn.

⚜ In a large sauté pan over medium heat cook the onion and red pepper in the canola oil until soft. Add garlic, horseradish, and cream. Cut corn off the cobs and add the kernels to the pan. Milk the corn cobs by scraping them firmly with the back of a knife and add the corn milk to the cream mixture. Simmer the cream mixture until it thickens slightly, about 8 minutes. Season with salt and pepper and keep warm.

⚜ To prepare the oysters, shuck the oysters, reserving the bottoms of the oyster shells; add oyster liquor to the corn sauce. Add oil in a deep pan to a depth of 3 inches; heat over medium-high heat until oil registers 350°F on a deep-fat thermometer, or until it shimmers. Season the oysters with salt and pepper, then dredge in blue cornmeal and fry until golden, 2 to 3 minutes. Drain on paper towels.

⚜ To serve, place six oyster bottoms on each of 4 plates. Fill the bottoms with corn sauce. Top with oysters. Garnish with green onions and red pepper.

SERVES FOUR

Coconut-Crusted Rockfish with Green Curry–Lemongrass Sauce

Brett Knipmeyer, Kinley's

The Pacific rockfish is respected among culinarians for its sweet, white meat that is similar to sea bass. The fish gained notoriety in 2007 when one that scientists believed to be at least 100 years old was caught south of the Pribilof Islands.

GREEN CURRY–LEMONGRASS SAUCE

One 13-ounce can coconut milk

1 stalk lemongrass, roughly chopped

1 tablespoon plus 1 teaspoon green curry paste

1 tablespoon rice vinegar

1 teaspoon honey

¼ teaspoon salt

COCONUT-CRUSTED ROCKFISH

1½-pound rockfish fillet

Salt and freshly ground black pepper

2 eggs

¼ cup half-and-half

1 cup panko (Japanese bread crumbs, available in Asian markets and some supermarkets)

1 cup flaked coconut, lightly toasted

1 cup all-purpose flour

Canola oil for frying

VEGETABLE SAUTÉ

1 carrot, julienned

1 teaspoon canola oil

1 teaspoon sesame oil

1 baby bok choy, julienned

1 red bell pepper, julienned

1 teaspoon minced garlic

1 teaspoon minced shallot

Salt and freshly ground black pepper

    ¼ cup thinly sliced green onion

    2 tablespoons minced parsley

✦ To make the lemongrass sauce, in a small saucepan bring the coconut milk, lemongrass, green curry paste, vinegar, and honey to a gentle simmer for 30 minutes. Strain and add salt; keep warm.

✦ To prepare the rockfish, cut the fillet into 8 portions and season with salt and pepper. In a small bowl, combine eggs and half-and-half. In another bowl, combine panko and coconut. Dredge rockfish portions in flour, dip in egg wash, then press into panko mixture; reserve.

✦ In a large skillet, add enough canola oil to come halfway up the thickest portion of the rockfish; heat oil over medium-high heat until it shimmers. Add fish pieces in single layer, cook until golden; flip, cook until other side is golden, about 2 minutes on each side. Drain on paper towels. Keep warm.

✦ To make the vegetable sauté, blanch the carrots in simmering water for 1 minute, strain, shock in ice water, and pat dry. In a large pan heat canola and sesame oils; sauté carrot, bok choy, and red pepper for 1 minute, then add garlic and shallot. Toss once, then season with salt and pepper.

✦ To serve, divide sauce among 4 plates. Top with fried rockfish and garnish with green onion and parsley. Serve with the vegetable sauté.

    SERVES FOUR

Roulade of Yellowfin Tuna Tartare

Jens Hansen, Jens' Restaurant

The quality of fish in Alaska—even fish shipped in—is usually so good that eating it raw never raises an eyebrow. Make sure the fish you buy is fresh and clean-smelling. Note: A mandoline is a manually operated slicer used in professional kitchens. Similar slicers made of plastic with stainless steel blades may be found in most kitchen shops.

2 pounds sushi grade yellowfin (ahi) tuna, roughly chopped
1 green mango, peeled and chopped
2 tablespoons ketchup
1 teaspoon hot sesame oil
1 tablespoon Thai fish sauce
6 green onions, thinly sliced
1 tablespoon whole cumin seeds, toasted
3 tablespoons prepared wasabi
3 tablespoons peeled and grated fresh horseradish
2 English cucumbers
Arugula leaves
Smoked Alaskan salmon caviar or other caviar (optional)
Rose petals (optional)

- To make the tartare filling, mix the tuna, mango, ketchup, hot sesame oil, Thai fish sauce, green onions, and cumin seeds in a large bowl. Refrigerate.

- In a small bowl, mix together the wasabi and horseradish. Set aside.

- Trim the ends from the cucumbers, then slice thin with a mandoline or similar slicer. Lightly brush 1 one side of each cucumber slice with the wasabi-horseradish mixture. Spread some tuna mixture on each cucumber slice. Roll the tuna-topped cucumber slices into rolls. Place on a pan and cover with plastic wrap. Freeze for 15 minutes.

- To serve, place arugula leaves on a chilled plate. Place the tartare rolls on the leaves. Dot with caviar and sprinkle rose petals over, if desired. Serve.

SERVES SIX AS A MAIN COURSE OR TWELVE AS AN APPETIZER

Salmon Belly Lasagna

Laura Cole, 229 Parks Restaurant and Tavern

This is a great way to turn salmon belly trim into an elegant dish. The chard filling elevates it to the sublime, especially if you get the chard after the first frost, when the sugars are intensified, giving the chard a wonderful sweet, earthy flavor.

LASAGNA NOODLES

½ cup organic semolina flour
½ cup organic unbleached all-purpose flour
Pinch of kosher salt
2 tablespoons chopped fresh thyme
1 free-range egg
2-plus tablespoons water

SWISS CHARD FILLING

1 tablespoon organic extra-virgin olive oil
8 cups chopped organic Swiss chard, beet greens, or a combination
Sea salt (preferably Maldon) and freshly ground pepper

LASAGNA

2 tablespoons unsalted butter, melted
1½ cups organic heavy cream
2 cups crumbled goat cheese
2 cups skinless salmon belly strips or quality salmon trim
Sea salt (preferably Maldon) and freshly ground pepper

✢ To make the lasagna noodles, combine the semolina flour, all-purpose flour, salt, and thyme in a large mixing bowl. Mix in the egg and water. Knead either by machine or by hand: dough should be the consistency of slightly grainy Play-Doh. Pass the dough through a pasta machine, beginning with the widest setting (#7). Then pass the dough through two settings smaller (#5). Repeat again two settings smaller (#3). Use immediately or prepare for freezing. To freeze, lay one layer of pasta sheets on a small baking pan lined with plastic wrap. Cover with plastic wrap and repeat with another layer. Repeat until all sheets are wrapped.

✦ To make the Swiss chard filling, heat the olive oil in a large sauté pan over high heat until it shimmers. Add the chard, season with salt and pepper, and remove from heat. Stir the chard until it is well coated. (The residual heat from the pan will finish the cooking process.) Stir from time to time until the chard is wilted. Adjust seasoning.

✦ To make the lasagna, preheat the oven to 350°F. Butter an 8-inch square oven-proof baking dish with 1 tablespoon of the melted butter. Place one layer of prepared noodles in dish. Mix the cream and 1 cup of the goat cheese. Add half of the goat cheese–cream mixture on top of the layer of pasta. Top with salmon belly. Season with salt and pepper. Add the Swiss chard filling and sprinkle with the remaining goat cheese, then cover with remaining goat cheese–cream mixture. Finish with a layer of pasta. Brush pasta with the remaining tablespoon of melted butter. Cover with plastic wrap and then with aluminum foil (the plastic protects the lasagna from the foil). Bake for 25 minutes, remove foil and plastic wrap, and return lasagna to the oven for 10 minutes to slightly crisp the top layer of pasta.

SERVES SIX

Mesquite Prawns with Mandarin Orange–Cilantro Sauce

Michele Camera-Faurot, Cafe Michele

This new addition to Cafe Michele's menu has been a great hit. The pungent mesquite set against the deep sweetness of the reduced orange–cilantro blend is a cooling and luscious combination.

MANDARIN ORANGE–CILANTRO SAUCE

Five 11-ounce cans of mandarin oranges in juice

¼ cup chopped fresh cilantro

1 teaspoon minced fresh ginger

1 teaspoon minced garlic

½ teaspoon orange zest

1 teaspoon sesame oil

PRAWNS

4 tablespoons Clarified Butter (page 203)

1½ pounds large prawns (under 15 per pound), peeled and deveined

½ cup mesquite seasoning

Cooked jasmine rice

✢ To make the sauce, simmer oranges until reduced by three-quarters; be careful not to burn. Remove from heat and stir in cilantro, ginger, garlic, orange zest, and sesame oil. Keep warm.

✢ To prepare the prawns, heat butter in large sauté pan over medium-high heat. Season the prawns with mesquite seasoning on one side only. Place the prawns, seasoned side down, in the sauté pan and cook for 1 minute. Turn the prawns and cook for another minute. Serve prawns over jasmine rice and top with mandarin orange sauce.

SERVES FOUR

Italian-Style King Crab with Basil Butter

Michele Camera-Faurot, Cafe Michele

Camera-Faurot's daughter, Gabby, adores king crab legs. This preparation was invented as a treat for her and never fails to produce a big smile.

BASIL BUTTER

1 cup (2 sticks) unsalted butter, softened
¼ cup chopped fresh basil
1 teaspoon lemon zest
Pinch of salt
Pinch of pepper

ITALIAN-STYLE KING CRAB

Twenty 4- to 5-inch king crab legs
Olive oil to coat
1 cup dry bread crumbs
2 tablespoons melted unsalted butter
¼ cup grated Romano cheese
2 tablespoons chopped parsley
¼ teaspoon salt
Pinch of pepper

✦ To make the basil butter, melt butter and stir in basil, lemon zest, salt, and pepper. Keep warm.

✦ To prepare the crab, preheat the oven to 400°F. Brush each crab leg completely with olive oil. In a medium bowl, mix bread crumbs, butter, Romano, parsley, salt, and pepper. Lightly pack bread crumb mixture on the meat of each crab leg. Transfer the legs to a baking pan and roast for 12 to 14 minutes. Remove and serve with basil butter for dipping.

SERVES FOUR

Coconut Curry Seafood Rice Bowl

Michele Camera-Faurot, Cafe Michele

Indian cooking features many curry blends, but Madras is Camera-Faurot's favorite. This curry is mild and has a coconut finish. At Cafe Michele it is also offered with tofu or grilled free-range chicken breast. Madras curry sauce can be found in the Indian section of your grocery store.

COCONUT CURRY

Four 13.1-ounce cans coconut milk
1½ tablespoons finely chopped fresh ginger
1½ tablespoons finely chopped garlic
12-inch piece of lemongrass, cut into 2-inch pieces
½ cup Madras curry sauce, or 3 tablespoons Madras curry paste
Salt

SEAFOOD RICE BOWL

½ cup ½-inch cubes fresh halibut
½ cup ½-inch cubes fresh king salmon
½ cup bay scallops
½ cup peeled and deveined Alaskan spot shrimp (or medium shrimp)
1 cup blanched broccoli florets
1 cup blanched ¼-inch-thick half-moon carrot slices
½ cup thinly sliced leek
¼ cup thinly sliced red onion
1 cup thinly sliced celery
½ cup ½-inch diced yellow squash
½ cup ½-inch diced zucchini
1 cup snow peas cut in half on the diagonal
3 cups cooked jasmine rice
¼ cup chopped cilantro

✧ To make the coconut curry, in a saucepan over medium heat, reduce coconut milk by two-thirds. Turn off heat, add ginger, garlic, lemongrass, and curry. Let steep until liquid is cool. Remove and discard lemongrass. Season with salt. Refrigerate (it will keep for 1 week in a tightly sealed container).

✦ To make the seafood rice bowl, add the coconut curry to a large pan and bring to a simmer. Add halibut, salmon, scallops, and shrimp. Simmer for 3 minutes. Add broccoli, carrots, leek, red onion, celery, squash, zucchini, and snow peas. Cook until the squash is just tender, about 3 minutes. Serve over jasmine rice divided among 4 warm, large bowls. Sprinkle with cilantro.

SERVES FOUR

Pan-Seared Beef Tenderloin with Pinot Noir Sauce and Mushroom Strudel

Farrokh Larijani, Glacier BrewHouse

Despite the abundance of seafood and the recent influence of cooking styles from Asia, California, and the Mediterranean, Alaskans love meat and potatoes. This recipe plays off that love of good beef but adds a little sophistication. Although this is labor-intensive, it is a great dish for a dinner party.

MUSHROOM STRUDEL

8 ounces portobello mushrooms

2 tablespoons butter

¼ cup diced (¼ inch) shallots

4 ounces medium button mushrooms, diced ¼ inch

2 teaspoons roughly chopped fresh oregano

1 teaspoon finely chopped rosemary

1 tablespoon roughly chopped basil

½ teaspoon kosher salt

½ teaspoon freshly ground black pepper

½ cup bread crumbs

4 egg roll wrappers (available in Asian markets)

2 eggs, beaten

PINOT NOIR SAUCE

2 tablespoons olive oil

2 tablespoons chopped shallots

1 clove garlic, chopped

¼ cup chopped mushrooms

1 teaspoon chopped dried mushrooms

1 tablespoon chopped sun-dried tomatoes

1 tablespoon balsamic vinegar

½ cup pinot noir

1 bay leaf

1 sprig of thyme, chopped

1 tablespoon chopped basil

½ teaspoon freshly cracked black pepper

1½ cups demi-glace (available in specialty food shops)

1 teaspoon arrowroot

1 tablespoon water

TENDERLOIN

2 leeks, white and light green parts

Vegetable oil, for frying

20 ounces trimmed beef tenderloin

¾ teaspoon kosher salt

¼ teaspoon freshly ground black pepper

4 tablespoons olive oil

4 tablespoons (½ stick) butter

20 spears fresh asparagus, steamed and kept warm

⚜ To make the mushroom strudels, scrape the black gills off the portobello mushrooms with a spoon and remove the stems. Cut the mushroom caps and stems in ¼-inch dice. Heat the butter in a heavy skillet over medium-high heat until it foams. Add the shallots and portobello and button mushrooms. Sauté until cooked through, about 3 minutes. Remove from the heat, then stir in the oregano, rosemary, basil, salt, pepper, and bread crumbs. Allow mixture to cool to room temperature.

⚜ Lay the egg roll wrappers out on a clean work surface. Spread the mushroom mixture evenly over the wrappers, leaving 1 inch free space on the wrapper on the edge away from you. Brush the free space with beaten egg. Beginning with the side near you, roll the wrapper, jelly-roll style, into a tight cylinder. Place the 4 cylinders on a greased baking tray, seam side down. Set aside.

⚜ To make the pinot noir sauce, heat the olive oil in a heavy saucepan over medium-high heat until it shimmers. Add the shallots, garlic, and chopped mushrooms and sauté for 3 minutes. Add the dried mushrooms and sun-dried tomatoes and stir until incorporated. Add the balsamic vinegar and reduce by half.

⚜ Add the pinot noir, bay leaf, thyme, basil, and pepper and reduce by half. Add the demi-glace and simmer for 10 minutes. Make a slurry of the arrowroot and water. Whipping constantly, add the slurry to the sauce in a steady stream. Simmer 5 minutes. Strain and keep warm.

⚜ Preheat the oven to 400°F.

✦ Cut the leeks lengthwise into thin strips, then wash well. Pat dry. Heat the vegetable oil in a Dutch oven or deep-fat fryer to 350°F. Fry the leeks until golden brown, remove, and drain on paper towels. Set aside.

✦ Bake the strudels until golden brown. Remove and keep warm.

✦ To prepare the tenderloin, cut it into 8 equal medallions. Season with the salt and pepper. Heat the olive oil in a heavy sauté pan until it just begins to smoke. Sear the medallions on both sides until browned. Remove and keep warm. Turn the heat off on the stove. Discard the remaining oil in the pan. Add 1½ cups of the pinot noir sauce, scraping any browned bits off the bottom of the pan with a wooden spoon. Swirl in the butter. Keep warm.

✦ Cut the strudels in half diagonally. Stack the asparagus in the center of 4 large, warm dinner plates. Shingle 2 medallions on top of the asparagus. Arrange the 2 halves of a strudel next to the medallions. Drizzle a bit of sauce over the medallions and the remaining sauce all over the plates. Place a haystack of fried leeks on top of the medallions and serve.

SERVES FOUR

Moose

Moose doesn't show up on restaurant menus in Alaska, but the rich meat is as much a part of the state's table as salmon. Hunters take more than seven thousand moose each year. A mature male can weigh more than 1,500 pounds and cows half a ton. That breaks down to as much as 700 pounds of edible meat. Imagine the freezer space you'd need!

In urban areas, neighborhood potlucks are built around pots of moose chili or pans of lasagna made with sweet, lean moose meat. Even families that don't have a hunter can usually get meat from a friend. Or, if they're particularly industrious and have tools for butchering, they can wait for a moose to get hit crossing a highway. Hundreds of the animals die that way each year, and the state keeps a list of people waiting their turn to salvage the meat.

In rural areas, where trips to the grocery store are infrequent or impossible, moose meat means survival. Meat is frozen or dried into jerky. Heads are boiled into soup and even the nose is eaten. Boiled until it is soft, it's considered quite a delicacy.

Some Alaska Natives rely on wild food such as moose for as much as half of their diet. Hunters share the choice parts of a moose with elders and others in the village. The animal is so much a part of Native life that cooks at the new, state-of-the-art Alaska Native Hospital in Anchorage simmer up batches of moose soup. For the hospital's patients, a bowl of moose broth is much more healing than chicken soup.

—Kim Severson

Pork Tenderloin with Birch Syrup–Mustard Sauce

Laura Cole, 229 Parks Restaurant and Tavern

The purpose of brining is to add subtle flavor and moisture to meat. When you brine meat, it absorbs the salt water. The salt in the brine denatures the meat's proteins, causing them to unwind and form a matrix that traps the brine solution. Some brines include sugars, spices, and seasonings. These, too, get trapped into the matrix of proteins. Brining carries flavor throughout the meat rather than just coating the surface. Adding sugar to a brine can balance the salt with sweetness and aid in caramelizing the meat's outer surface. Note: Birch syrup can be ordered from Kahiltna Birchworks in Alaska (see page 234), or you may substitute good-quality pure maple syrup.

BASIC BRINE

    2 cups water
    ¼ cup kosher salt
    ¼ cup birch syrup
    ¼ cup brown sugar
    1 clove garlic, crushed
    Leaves from 2 sprigs of rosemary
    Leaves from 3 sprigs of thyme
    1 tablespoon juniper berries, crushed

PORK TENDERLOIN

    2 free-range pork tenderloins, trimmed, silver skin removed
    2 tablespoons Alaskan birch syrup
    1 tablespoon Dijon mustard
    1 teaspoon freshly ground pepper
    1 teaspoon minced fresh rosemary
    1 teaspoon high-quality sea salt
    1 tablespoon extra-virgin olive oil

BIRCH SYRUP–MUSTARD SAUCE

    1 tablespoon Plugrá or other European-style butter
    ¼ cup minced leeks
    2 teaspoons minced fresh thyme
    ¼ cup unfiltered cider

1 cup roasted chicken broth (if purchased, use top-quality organic)
4 teaspoons birch syrup
2 tablespoons Dijon mustard
¼ cup heavy cream
Sea salt and freshly ground pepper

✢ To make the brine, in a medium saucepan combine water, salt, birch syrup, and brown sugar and bring to a simmer over medium-high heat. Stir until the sugar and salt are dissolved. Add garlic. Add rosemary and thyme leaves and juniper berries. Remove from heat, transfer the brine to a baking pan, and allow it to cool.

✢ To make the pork, add tenderloins to the brine and refrigerate for 10 to 12 hours. Preheat the oven to 400°F. Remove tenderloins from brine, pat dry. Combine the birch syrup and mustard, and brush onto the tenderloins. Mix together the pepper, rosemary, and salt. Sprinkle mixture over tenderloins. Heat olive oil in an ovenproof sauté pan over medium-high heat until it shimmers. Brown tenderloins on all sides and transfer pan to oven. Roast for 10 to 15 minutes, or until internal temperature in the thickest part of the tenderloins registers 150°F when measured with an instant-read thermometer. Remove the meat from the pan, tent with foil, and let rest 10 minutes.

✢ To make the sauce, in a large saucepan over medium-low heat melt butter, add leeks, and cook until they soften, about 4 minutes. Add thyme and deglaze with cider. Add broth, birch syrup, and mustard. Bring to a simmer and reduce by half, about 8 minutes. Finish (impart flavor and richness) with cream and season with salt and pepper.

✢ To serve, slice the tenderloin on the bias (at an angle). Divide the pieces among 6 warm plates, layering the slices. Top with syrup-mustard sauce.

SERVES SIX

Juniper-Rubbed Cornish Hens (or Guinea Hens)

Laura Cole, 229 Parks Restaurant and Tavern

Juniper grows wild all over interior Alaska. You can harvest and dry it on sheet trays for use throughout the year. The pancetta offers both a welcome bite of crispness and a protective cover for the delicate breast meat.

½ cup organic sugar

3 tablespoons kosher salt

4 teaspoons freshly ground black pepper

¼ cup fresh juniper berries, or 3 tablespoons dried, soaked for 3 hours and drained

4 cloves garlic

2 tablespoons fresh lemon juice

⅓ cup extra-virgin olive oil

4 small free-range, organic game birds (guinea or Cornish hens)

8 fresh (or 6 dried) bay leaves

4 sprigs of thyme

Four ¼-inch slices lemon

8 slices pancetta

4 thick slices toasted sourdough bread

⚴ In a food processor, purée sugar, salt, pepper, juniper berries, garlic, lemon juice, and olive oil. Reserve. Pat the birds dry, including the cavities. Stuff the birds with bay leaves, thyme, and lemon slices. Coat the birds with the juniper paste, tucking a little inside the cavities as well. Let sit for up to 1 hour, then coat again with paste.

⚴ Preheat the oven to 375°F. Set a grill rack on a roasting pan and arrange the birds on the rack, breast side down, making sure that they are not touching. Roast for 20 minutes, remove from oven, and turn the birds breast side up. Wrap 2 slices of pancetta over each breast. Continue to roast the birds, checking every 15 minutes, until an instant-read thermometer registers 165°F. Remove, tent with foil, and let rest for 8 minutes.

⚴ To serve, place the birds on top of the toasted sourdough bread (as you cut into it, the sourdough will soak up the wonderful juices rendered from the bird).

SERVES FOUR

Roast Cornish Hen with King Prawns

Al Levinsohn, Kincaid Grill

In Alaska, spot prawns come into season in April and are available fresh until October. This dish takes Alaska's best prawns and mixes them with a game bird. What a terrific surprise to find a tender prawn nestled inside a Cornish hen. Call it an Alaskan twist on the old surf and turf.

2 Cornish hens (22 to 24 ounces each)
2 cups Chicken Stock (page 194) or canned chicken broth
4 large (10 per pound) prawns or 8 smaller Alaskan spot prawns
½ cup cilantro, chopped
½ cup purple or sweet basil leaves, chopped
4 cloves garlic, sliced thin
1 tablespoon minced fresh ginger
2 teaspoons low-sodium soy sauce
2 tablespoons olive oil
1 tablespoon fresh lemon juice
Salt and freshly ground black pepper
¾ cup julienned carrot
¾ cup julienned celery
¾ cup julienned onion
2 Japanese eggplant, cut in half lengthwise
1 tablespoon olive oil
1 tablespoon rice vinegar
1 teaspoon *sambal oelek* (Thai chile sauce, available at Asian markets)
1 tablespoon cilantro leaves, minced

⚜ Remove the giblets, rinse the hens well under cool water, and pat dry. Cut the hens in half with a heavy knife or poultry shears. Cut off the wing tips and the tip joint of the legs. Carefully remove all the bones from each half of the hen without piercing the skin and flesh.

⚜ Add the giblets (except the livers), necks, wing tips, and tip joints to the chicken stock. Simmer over medium heat until reduced by one-quarter. Strain and reserve the resulting stock.

⚜ Lay the hen halves on the work surface, skin side down. Distribute the cilantro and basil equally over the cavities of the hens.

+ Peel the prawns, except for the tail, and devein. From the inside of the hen, run the tail of the prawn through the empty leg socket until the tail shell protrudes from the end. For smaller prawns, use two.

+ Mix together the garlic, ginger, soy sauce, olive oil, lemon juice, ½ teaspoon of salt, and a pinch of pepper in a small bowl. Equally divide the mixture, spreading it on top of the cilantro-basil layer in the cavity. Wrap the hen flesh around the prawn to form a package and tie with twine to hold its shape. Wrap the tail of the prawn with foil to protect it during the cooking process.

+ Preheat the oven to 350°F.

+ Place the hens in a Dutch oven or large, heavy cast-iron skillet so they don't touch. Roast for 20 minutes.

+ Meanwhile, toss the carrot, celery, onion, and eggplant in olive oil and rice vinegar and season with ¼ teaspoon salt, and a pinch of pepper.

+ Remove the hens from the oven and place the eggplants, skin side up, around them. Sprinkle the other vegetables on top of the hens and eggplant. Pour in ½ cup of the simmering stock, cover the pan, and return to the oven for 10 minutes more or until the hens and prawns are cooked through.

+ Remove the pan from the oven, move the eggplant on top of the hens, and add the *sambal oelek* and remaining simmering stock. The pan should be hot enough for the stock to reduce slightly. Add the cilantro. Remove the foil from the prawn tails.

+ Spoon the eggplant, skin side down, on a warm plate. Top with the other vegetables. Remove the hens and cut off the string. For each serving, slice the hen on the bias and arrange on top of the vegetables. Drizzle the outer plate area with the pan sauce, garnish with cilantro sprigs, and serve.

SERVES FOUR

Smoked Goose Pies

Kirsten Dixon, Within the Wild Lodges

This is definitely winter fare, although Dixon does the pot pie theme throughout the year. A prepared demi-glace may be cut in half with chicken stock to make a good, all-purpose stock when you can't make your own.

4 sheets (5 inches square) frozen puff pastry
3 tablespoons fresh thyme leaves
Coarsely ground sea salt
2 large carrots, peeled
2 medium Yukon Gold potatoes, scrubbed and quartered
2 large yellow onions, peeled and quartered
Extra-virgin olive oil
Freshly ground black pepper
1 cup Beef Stock (page 195), made with beef or veal
2 smoked goose breasts (see page 234)

⁜ Preheat the oven to 375°F.

⁜ Sprinkle the puff pastry sheets with 2 tablespoons of the thyme and sea salt. Bake in the oven until puffed and browned, about 7 minutes. Separate the top of the puff pastry from the bottom. Discard the bottoms and set the tops aside.

⁜ Cut off the tops and bottoms of the carrots to make them the same size. Cut the carrots in half lengthwise. Coat the carrots, potatoes, and onions lightly with olive oil, season with salt and pepper, and sprinkle with 2 tablespoons of the thyme. Place in a roasting pan. Roast until tender, checking after 20 minutes. Remove the vegetables as they are cooked and set aside in a warm place.

⁜ Warm the beef stock in a saucepan until it steams. Adjust the heat to maintain the steam. Do not simmer.

⁜ Trim the goose breasts of all fat. Thinly slice the breasts against the grain and gently stir into the steaming stock.

⁜ To assemble, warm 4 wide-rimmed bowls. Place ½ carrot, 2 potato quarters, and 2 onion quarters in each. Divide the goose meat, laying it across the vegetables in each of the bowls. Drizzle the stock remaining in the saucepan over the meat and vegetables. Sprinkle with remaining 1 teaspoon of thyme. Top the dish with a puff pastry top and serve.

SERVES FOUR

Hunter's Pot

Kirsten Dixon, Within the Wild Lodges

Dixon got the inspiration for this dish on a visit to Alain Ducasse's Le Louis XV in Monte Carlo. She was treated to a tour of the kitchen—not one single woman anywhere. The chef had large, twenty-five-pound bags of fleur de sel, a sea salt sold only in small precious jars in Alaska. She loves to serve this dish in the winter to buffalo hunters or wayward travelers along the Iditarod Trail. She uses wide-rimmed white pasta bowls so the dish isn't too crowded. You can buy the specialty meats at Alaska Game Sales (see page 234).

4 slices sourdough bread, crust trimmed
12 ounces Swiss chard
4 carrots, peeled and cut into thick matchsticks
4 parsnips, peeled and cut into thick matchsticks
Salt and freshly ground black pepper
2 tablespoons grapeseed oil
1 pound venison sausage
1 pound rabbit tenderloin or loin
1 pound reindeer or venison tenderloin
1 tablespoon butter
8 ounces foie gras, minced and chilled
2 cups Rabbit Foie Gras Jus (recipe follows)

✣ Preheat the oven to 350°F.

✣ Toast the bread until crisp and set aside.

✣ Season the carrots and parsnips with a sprinkling of salt and pepper. Place in a baking dish with enough water to cover the bottom of the dish. Cover with aluminum foil. Bake until tender, 30 to 40 minutes. Set aside.

✣ While the vegetables are baking, clean the chard and separate the leaves from the stems. Mince the stems and cut the leaves into thin strips.

✣ Heat a small sauté pan over medium heat and add 1 tablespoon of the grapeseed oil. Sauté the chard stems and set aside.

✣ Place the venison sausage in the oven and roast until hot throughout. Don't fry venison sausage or it will become too dry. Set aside in a warm place.

✦ Rub the rabbit and reindeer tenderloins with salt and pepper. Pan-sear the tenderloins in the remaining tablespoon of grapeseed oil in a medium pan over medium-high heat. Transfer the tenderloins to the oven and finish cooking. Set aside in a warm place.

✦ Steam the chard leaves, then toss with the butter. Season with salt and pepper. Set aside in a warm place.

✦ Sear the foie gras quickly on each side in a very hot pan; do this fast or the foie gras will melt. Spoon the foie gras and any drippings equally among the cooked toasts.

✦ Heat 4 wide-rimmed bowls. Place 1 toast in the center of each bowl. Slice the sausage, rabbit, and deer. Layer the meats on top of the foie gras. Top with the carrots, parsnips, and chard leaves. Nest the chard stems on the side of each toast.

✦ Ladle the rabbit foie gras jus over the top and serve.

SERVES FOUR

Rabbit Foie Gras Jus

This luscious liquid is a fine match for Dixon's Hunter's Pot, but it would also be a stellar compliment to any roasted game.

3 tablespoons olive oil
1 cup (2 sticks) butter
4½ pounds rabbit scraps and trim, any meat cut into ½-inch cubes
3 carrots
1 head garlic, cut in half
1 stalk celery, trimmed and chopped
Salt and freshly ground pepper
1 ounce foie gras, minced

✦ Heat the olive oil in a large stockpot over medium-high heat. Add the butter, allow it to melt, add the rabbit, and stir to coat. Add the carrots, garlic, celery, salt, and pepper. Cook until the rabbit is browned, then remove the meat and vegetables from the pot. Set aside.

✦ Add 1 cup of water to the pot and scrape up all of the browned bits remaining on the bottom of the pan. Simmer the water mixture until almost completely evaporated.

✦ Return the meat-vegetable mixture to the pot and cover with cold water. Bring the water to a boil, then reduce the heat to maintain a simmer. Simmer for 3 hours.

✦ Remove the meat and vegetables and discard. Strain the jus.

MAKES 5 CUPS

King Fredrik's Favorite Danish-Style Hash

Jens Hansen, Jens' Restaurant

King Fredrik must have been a pretty bright fellow. This hash is easy to prepare, yet very elegant and delicious. It reflects Hansen's simple but rich style of cooking. Its hearty nature is typical of how many Alaskan chefs cook.

½ cup Clarified Butter (page 203)
2 cups peeled and diced baking potatoes
1½ cups diced onion
12 ounces trimmed beef tenderloin, diced small
½ cup demi-glace (available in specialty food shops)
2 tablespoons Worcestershire sauce
Salt and freshly ground black pepper
4 fried eggs
½ cup chopped parsley

✦ In a large sauté pan over medium-high heat, heat one third of the butter until it is hot. Add the potatoes and cook until tender. Remove and keep warm.

✦ Add another third of the butter to the sauté pan and heat over medium heat until hot. Add the onions and cook until soft. Remove and keep warm.

✦ Add the remaining butter to the sauté pan and heat over medium-high heat until very hot. Add the tenderloin pieces and cook to the desired doneness. Drain any residual fat. Return the cooked potatoes and onions to the pan. Add the demi-glace and Worcestershire and toss to combine all the ingredients. Season with salt and pepper to taste.

✦ Divide the hot meat mixture among 4 warm plates. Top each with a fried egg. Garnish with parsley and serve.

SERVES FOUR

Migas with Avocado-Tomatillo Sauce

Alev Manalp, Sacks Cafe

Ever since the Russians arrived in the territory in the 1700s, immigrants have influenced food in Alaska. Anchorage has a small but active Latino community and several good cooks whose families come from Mexico. This lovely traditional dish would make a good start to the day or a perfect late-evening meal, served with warm corn tortillas.

AVOCADO-TOMATILLO SAUCE

2 cloves garlic, minced

5 medium tomatillos, peeled and washed

1 jalapeño, chopped (seeded if you like mild sauce)

½ cup chopped cilantro

1 ripe avocado

Salt

MIGAS

1 medium red bell pepper, sliced thin

1 medium red onion, finely diced

2 small jalapeños, finely diced (seeded if you like mild migas)

4 cloves garlic, minced

4 tomatoes, cored and diced small

Salt

2 tablespoons vegetable oil

¾ pound chorizo sausage, crumbled

10 eggs, beaten

½ cup grated sharp cheddar

½ cup grated Monterey Jack

½ cup chopped cilantro

✤ To make the avocado-tomatillo sauce, put all the ingredients in a food processor and pulse until chunky.

✤ To make the migas, combine the bell pepper, red onion, jalapeños, garlic, tomatoes, and ½ teaspoon of salt. Heat the vegetable oil in a large, heavy skillet until it shimmers. Sauté the chorizo until it is browned. Add the vegetable mixture and continue to cook until the onions and peppers just begin to soften. Add the eggs and stir constantly until cooked to desired consistency. Add the cheddar, Monterey Jack, and the cilantro and stir until cheeses are melted. Taste and adjust the seasoning with salt.

✤ Divide the migas among 4 hot plates and serve with the tomatillo sauce.

SERVES FOUR

Pan-Roasted Chicken Breasts with Chèvre-Herb Stuffing

Farrokh Larijani, Glacier BrewHouse

In a world packed with chicken breast recipes, this recipe stands out. The goat cheese stuffing not only adds flavor, it also contributes moisture to the breast.

FOCACCIA CROUTONS

2 tablespoons butter

4 focaccia, cut into 3-inch circles

CHÈVRE-HERB STUFFING

4 tablespoons butter, salted

3 ounces chèvre

2 cloves garlic, minced

2 tablespoons chopped basil

1 teaspoon minced fresh thyme

½ teaspoon chopped fresh marjoram

½ teaspoon minced rosemary

1 tablespoon thinly sliced green onion

3 tablespoons grated Parmesan

Pinch of crushed red pepper

¼ teaspoon coarsely ground black pepper

½ teaspoon granulated onion

½ teaspoon granulated garlic

½ teaspoon kosher salt

CHICKEN BREASTS

4 chicken breasts, skin on (5 ounces each)

1 tablespoon chopped fresh thyme

1 tablespoon chopped rosemary

1 tablespoon chopped sage

1 tablespoon chopped fresh oregano

1 teaspoon crushed red pepper

1 teaspoon kosher salt

4 tablespoons olive oil

3 cups small-diced onion

⅓ cup small-diced roasted red pepper

¾ cup Chicken Stock (page 194) or canned chicken broth

1 tablespoon fresh lemon juice

1 teaspoon freshly ground black pepper

✢ To make the croutons, melt the butter and sauté the focaccia over moderate heat until golden brown. Set aside.

✢ To make the chèvre-herb stuffing, process all the ingredients in a food processor until smooth. Scrape down the sides. Process again until smooth. Refrigerate. Soften slightly for use.

✢ Preheat the oven to 350°F.

✢ Trim the fat from the chicken breasts. Insert 1½ tablespoons of the stuffing between the skin and flesh of each chicken breast. Mix together the thyme, rosemary, sage, oregano, red pepper, and salt. Sprinkle 1 tablespoon of the herb mix on top of each breast. Refrigerate.

✢ Heat the olive oil in a heavy ovenproof pan until it shimmers. Sear the chicken, skin side down, until golden. Turn the chicken over, place the pan in the oven, and roast until cooked through, 12 to 15 minutes. Check with a paring knife to ensure that there is no pink. Remove the chicken and keep warm.

✢ Drain any excess oil from the pan and add the onion and red pepper. Add the chicken stock and lemon juice and whisk in the remaining stuffing. Season with black pepper, place on medium-high heat, and simmer until the liquid is almost entirely reduced.

✢ Place the croutons on 4 warm plates and pour the pan sauce equally over all of the croutons, letting the sauce pool onto the plate. Top with the cooked chicken breasts and serve.

SERVES FOUR

Pan-Seared Duck Breasts with Alaskan Lowbush Cranberry Port Au Jus

Brett Custer, The Homestead Restaurant

Fresh duck breasts are readily available at the market these days. If whole duck is your only choice, have your butcher bone out the breasts and remove the legs and thighs from the carcass (use this to make the stock). The legs and thighs may be either slow-roasted or braised to accompany these breasts to the table. Dried cranberries may be substituted for the lowbush cranberries.

ALASKAN LOWBUSH CRANBERRY PORT AU JUS

> 3 cups Roasted Duck Stock (page 198)
> 1 cup port
> ½ cup lowbush cranberries
> Salt and freshly ground black pepper

DUCK BREASTS

> 4 organic duck breasts
> Salt and freshly ground black pepper
> 1 tablespoon canola oil

⁜ To make the au jus, combine the duck stock, port, and cranberries in a large saucepan. Bring to a simmer and cook until liquid has been reduced by three-quarters, about 20 minutes. Season with salt and pepper. Keep warm.

⁜ To prepare the duck, preheat the oven to 400°F. Score the fat layer of the duck breasts four times. Season breasts on fat side with salt and pepper. Heat canola oil over high heat in an ovenproof sauté pan until almost smoking. Carefully add the duck breasts, fat side down. Cook until the fat is well-browned and crisp, about 4 minutes; discard excess oil. Turn the breasts over and place pan in the oven for 3 to 5 minutes. Remove breasts from pan and let rest, covered with foil, for 5 minutes. Slice breasts.

⁜ To serve, divide duck breast slices among 4 warm plates, layering them and pouring a ribbon of au jus over each portion.

SERVES FOUR

Braised Lamb Shanks with Sweet-and-Sour Onions

Farrokh Larijani, Glacier BrewHouse

Lamb shanks, long neglected by many cooks in the United States, have come into their own. Braising ensures a tender, succulent result for this cut of lamb. Larijani provides an exciting surprise of flavors with the onion garnish. Polenta is a natural match for this dish. Note: If red pearl onions are unavailable, increase yellow pearl onions to 2 cups.

BRAISING LIQUID

8 cups unsalted Chicken Stock (page 194) or canned chicken broth

1 sprig of rosemary

2 sprigs of thyme

4 cloves roasted garlic

2 cups Beef Stock (page 195) or canned beef broth

LAMB SHANKS

4 lamb shanks (12 ounces each)

1 tablespoon kosher salt

1 teaspoon freshly ground black pepper

2 tablespoons vegetable oil

1 medium onion, chopped

2 stalks celery, chopped

1 cup chopped carrots

2 cups dry red wine

2 cloves garlic

1 bay leaf

½ teaspoon dried thyme leaves

SWEET-AND-SOUR ONIONS

½ cup white balsamic vinegar

3 tablespoons sugar

1 cup yellow pearl onions, blanched and peeled

1 cup red pearl onions, blanched and peeled (see Note)

GARNISH

       3 tablespoons olive oil

       4 Roma tomatoes, cored, seeded, and diced (½ inch)

       ½ cup Kalamata olives, pitted and quartered

       4 tablespoons thinly sliced basil

       1 teaspoon freshly ground black pepper

⊹ To prepare the braising liquid, combine the chicken stock, rosemary, thyme, and garlic in a large saucepan and bring to a boil. Reduce by three-quarters. Add the beef stock, then strain. Use the liquid for braising lamb shanks.

⊹ Preheat the oven to 350°F.

⊹ To prepare the lamb shanks, season with salt and pepper. Heat the vegetable oil in a heavy ovenproof pan or Dutch oven until it shimmers. Add the shanks and brown well on all sides. Add the onion, celery, and carrots and continue to brown over moderate heat. Add the red wine and reduce by half. Add the garlic, bay leaf, thyme, and 4 cups of the braising liquid, bring to a simmer, cover, and braise in the oven until the shanks are fork tender, about 2½ to 3 hours. Remove the shanks, cover, and set aside in a warm place. Strain the braising liquid and set aside.

⊹ To prepare the sweet-and-sour onions, bring the vinegar to a boil in a large skillet, add the sugar, and cook over medium-high heat until it is dissolved. Add the onions and continue to cook until the onions are well coated and caramelized. Remove from the skillet and allow onions to cool at room temperature. Set aside.

⊹ To prepare the garnish, heat the olive oil in a skillet until it starts to shimmer. Add the reserved onions, tomatoes, and olives. Toss just to heat through. Add 2 cups of the braising liquid and continue to cook until hot. Remove from the heat and add the basil and pepper. Taste to check for seasoning; a bit of salt may be required.

⊹ Place the lamb shanks on 4 warm plates. Spoon the garnish equally over each shank.

SERVES FOUR

Pistachio-Crusted Rack of Lamb with Port-Olive Sauce

Elizabeth King, Southside Bistro

In Anchorage, Alaska's biggest city, chefs often impress guests with surprising twists of sophistication. This is one of those dishes. A mustard meringue and the Kalamata olive sauce make it a memorable alternative to the standard rack of lamb. This dish is great with Goat Cheese Mashed Potatoes (page 176).

PORT-OLIVE SAUCE

    1 cup ruby Port

    1 teaspoon chopped garlic

    2 teaspoons chopped shallots

    1 sprig of rosemary

    Zest of 1 orange

    ⅔ cup demi-glace (available in specialty food shops)

    ¼ cup sliced Kalamata olives

    Salt and freshly ground black pepper

LAMB

    ⅓ cup shelled pistachios

    ½ cup panko (Japanese bread crumbs, available in Asian markets and some supermarkets)

    1 tablespoon chopped Italian parsley

    ¼ teaspoon salt

    Pinch of freshly ground black pepper

    2 racks of lamb, frenched (7 to 8 bones each)

    2 tablespoons olive oil

    2 egg whites

    Pinch of cream of tartar

    1 tablespoon Dijon mustard

    1 teaspoon fresh thyme leaves

⚜ Preheat the oven to 400°F.

⚜ To make the sauce, combine the Port, garlic, shallots, rosemary, and orange zest in a medium saucepan and simmer until the liquid is reduced by a third.

Strain and return the liquid to the saucepan. Add the demi-glace, bring to a boil, remove from heat, add olives, and season with salt and pepper.

✦ Combine the pistachios, panko, parsley, salt, and pepper in a food processor. Process until the nuts are chopped very fine.

✦ Wrap each bone of the lamb in aluminum foil to prevent burning and season the meat lightly with salt and pepper. Pour the olive oil into a very hot skillet, add the lamb, and sear all sides of the chops until browned, about 8 minutes; remove and allow lamb to cool.

✦ Put the egg whites and cream of tartar in a clean bowl and whip to stiff peaks. Fold in the mustard. Coat the top side of each rack with the mustard meringue. Press the pistachio mixture on top of meringue. Roast the racks to the desired doneness, about 15 minutes for rare. Allow racks to rest 10 minutes before carving. Remove aluminum foil from ribs. As the racks rest, reheat the sauce to a simmer. Add the fresh thyme. Carve racks into chops; pool sauce around and over, and serve.

SERVES FOUR

Rack of Lamb with Garlic, Rosemary, and Lemon Zest

Laura Cole, 229 Parks Restaurant and Tavern

The lovely flavor of young lamb is perfectly complemented by white beans and fresh tomatoes perfumed with rosemary and lemon zest.

Two 8-rib lamb racks, cut into 2-rib portions
Sea salt and freshly ground pepper
4 tablespoons extra-virgin olive oil
4 cloves garlic, minced
2 cups diced organic heirloom tomatoes
2 cups cooked organic white beans
3 tablespoons minced fresh rosemary
½ cup minced fresh parsley
2 cups fresh chicken broth
3 tablespoons fresh lemon zest

✢ Season lamb with salt and pepper. Heat 2 tablespoons of the olive oil in a large sauté pan over medium-high heat until it shimmers. Sear four 2-rib portions of the lamb, browning well on both sides, about 8 minutes. Remove, keep warm, and repeat with the remaining lamb until all pieces are seared, adding more oil as needed. Pour off and discard excess oil. Reduce heat, add garlic and tomatoes and cook, stirring, for about 2 minutes, or until you smell the aroma of garlic. Add beans, 2 tablespoons of the rosemary, and ¼ cup of the parsley. Simmer for 2 minutes. Add chicken broth, bring to a low simmer, stir in 2 tablespoons of the lemon zest, and top with reserved lamb. Simmer until most of the liquid has evaporated.

✢ To serve, divide the lamb among 4 warm plates. Stir the remaining rosemary, parsley, and lemon zest into the bean mixture. Top lamb with bean mixture.

SERVES FOUR

Grilled Skirt Steak with Tequila Vinaigrette

Farrokh Larijani, Glacier BrewHouse

Cool salad greens with untraditional garnishes, a unique dressing, and hot, flavorful steak fresh off of the grill topped with a great puréed salsa—this is a main course salad that seems at first glance to be very involved. In fact, the dish is quite simple and refreshing on a sunny barbecue day. It was inspired by Mike Jones, one of Larijani's cooks, who invented the salsa. Look for the smoked paprika at a Mexican grocery or specialty store.

MEAT RUB

2½ teaspoons kosher salt

½ teaspoon freshly ground black pepper

½ medium yellow onion, thinly sliced

2 tablespoons chopped cilantro

Juice of 1 lime

1 cup brown ale

2 tablespoons paprika (preferably smoked)

1 teaspoon puréed kiwi

1¾ pounds skirt steak or flank steak

TEQUILA VINAIGRETTE

2 tablespoons minced shallots

½ cup bottled margarita mix

½ teaspoon minced lime zest

½ tablespoon fresh lime juice

2 tablespoons tequila

1¼ teaspoons kosher salt

¼ teaspoon freshly ground black pepper

1 tablespoon chopped cilantro

½ cup vegetable oil

SALSA

3 medium tomatoes, cored, seeded, and chopped

4 cups water

¼ cup diced red bell pepper

¼ cup diced green bell pepper

4 jalapeños (seeded if you like mild salsa)

½ medium yellow onion, chopped

2 cloves garlic, chopped

½ teaspoon ground cumin

1½ teaspoons kosher salt

½ cup chopped cilantro

2 teaspoons fresh oregano leaves, minced

SALAD

4 cups salad greens

4 cups mesclun mix

¾ cup papaya and mango chunks

1¼ cups seeded Roma tomatoes, cut in large dice

½ cup thinly sliced red onion

8 baby corn (optional)

1 cup snow peas, cut into thin strips (optional)

✢ To make the meat rub, mix the salt, pepper, onion, cilantro, lime juice, ale, paprika, and kiwi to make a thin paste.

✢ Trim the steak of any fat. Rub the seasoning mixture onto all surfaces of the meat, cover, and refrigerate for 10 hours. Turn the meat over after 5 hours.

✢ To make the tequila vinaigrette, combine shallots, margarita mix, lime zest, lime juice, tequila, salt, pepper, and cilantro in a medium bowl and mix. Whisk in the vegetable oil in a thin, steady stream. Set aside.

✢ To make the salsa, place the tomatoes, water, bell peppers, jalapeños, onion, garlic, cumin, and salt in a large saucepan, bring to a boil, and cook until the water is reduced by two-thirds. Purée the reduced mixture in a food processor. Stir in the cilantro and oregano. Check seasoning for salt. Set aside.

✢ Preheat the grill.

✢ Remove the steak from the refrigerator. Grill the meat over hot coals until cooked to the desired doneness. Remove from the grill, tent with foil, and set aside in a warm place for 10 minutes before carving.

✢ Meanwhile, make the salad. Combine the salad greens, mesclun mix, papaya and mango, tomatoes, onion, corn, and snow peas. Toss with 1 cup of the vinaigrette, setting aside the remaining vinaigrette for another day. Divide the dressed salad among 4 plates.

✢ Slice the beef into thin strips at an angle across the grain of the meat. Arrange the meat around the salads. Spoon the salsa on top of the meat and serve.

SERVES FOUR

Stuffed Pork Chops with Oven-Roasted Herbed Tomatoes

Farrokh Larijani, Glacier BrewHouse

Polenta would be a great addition to these chops.

CURING BRINE

3 teaspoons crushed garlic cloves

4 cups water

3 tablespoons kosher salt

1 tablespoon sugar

½ teaspoon dried thyme

1 tablespoon black peppercorns

½ bay leaf

Pinch of mustard seeds

Pinch of crushed red pepper

Pinch of crushed star anise

PORK CHOPS

4 bone-in pork chops (12 ounces each)

8 ounces sweet Sicilian sausage or bulk Italian sausage, cooked

¼ cup thinly sliced basil

¼ cup brandy

1¼ cups Beef Stock (page 195) or high-quality canned beef broth

2 cups Oven-Roasted Herbed Tomatoes (page 177)

3 tablespoons pine nuts, toasted

4 sprigs of sage

↟ To make the curing brine, place all the ingredients into a pot and bring to a boil. Simmer for 10 minutes. Allow brine to cool. Refrigerate.

↟ Place the pork chops in the cold brine and refrigerate for 24 hours.

↟ Preheat the grill. Preheat the oven to 450°F.

↟ Remove the chops from the brine. Drain. With a boning knife or paring knife, cut a pocket into each chop. Stuff each chop with the cooked sausage and basil. Grill the chops for 3 minutes on each side, then place in an ovenproof sauté pan just large enough to hold them. Roast in the oven until an instant-read thermometer registers 155°F. Remove the chops from the pan, tent with aluminum foil, and keep warm.

✤ Place the sauté pan over medium-high heat and add the brandy. Scrape the pan with a wooden spoon to release drippings. Add the beef stock, bring to a boil, and reduce the mixture to a syrupy consistency.

✤ Place the chops on 4 warm plates and drizzle the pan sauce over the pork. Garnish with the tomatoes, pine nuts, and a sage sprig.

SERVES FOUR

Pork Medallions with Porter Applesauce

Brett Custer, The Homestead Restaurant

Custer made this dish to celebrate the folks at Homer Brewing Company, who help make living on the Kenai Peninsula even more fun. Any good porter will work in this great twist on traditional applesauce.

PORTER APPLESAUCE

6 Braeburn or Fuji apples, peeled, cored and finely diced

4 cups porter beer (preferably a Homer Brewing Company porter)

½ teaspoon ground allspice

½ teaspoon ground nutmeg

1 cup brown sugar

½ teaspoon salt

PORK MEDALLIONS

1½-pound pork tenderloin

Salt and freshly ground black pepper

3 ounces (1 cup) shredded aged white cheddar

✦ To make the applesauce, in a large saucepan simmer the apples, beer, allspice, nutmeg, brown sugar, and salt until the apples are just soft, not mushy, about 13 minutes. In a blender or food processor, briefly process the apple mixture, leaving the applesauce slightly chunky. Strain the applesauce through a fine mesh strainer, reserving liquid to adjust consistency before serving. If the applesauce is too bitter from the beer, add more brown sugar to taste. Season with salt. Keep warm.

✦ To prepare the pork, preheat a grill. Slice the pork into 12 equal pieces. Place the pork, cut side up, on a flat surface and cover with plastic wrap. Gently pound the pork slices with the flat side of a meat mallet or a skillet until they are ½ inch thick. Season each piece with salt and pepper. Grill to desired doneness, preferably medium or medium rare.

✦ To serve, divide the pork medallions equally among 4 dinner plates, layering medallions. Adjust consistency of applesauce. Top each portion with ¼ cup of the applesauce and sprinkle with the cheddar.

SERVES FOUR

Pan-Seared Venison Medallions
with Raspberry–Green Peppercorn Sauce

Elizabeth King, Southside Bistro

At the restaurant, they use farm-raised venison from New Zealand, but you can substitute your own game deer. Caribou or elk would also work well, as would veal. As an accompaniment, try Sweet Onion Jam (page 192) and Twice-Baked Gorgonzola Potatoes (page 175).

1½ pounds venison loin medallions
Kosher salt and freshly ground black pepper
1 tablespoon chopped fresh thyme
½ cup fresh or frozen unsweetened raspberries
1½ tablespoons dried green peppercorns
¾ cup ruby Port
3 tablespoons chopped shallots
¾ cup demi-glace (available in specialty food shops)
2 tablespoons olive oil
4 tablespoons butter, chilled, cut into 4 equal pieces

✦ Space out the medallions on a cutting board and cover with plastic wrap. Gently pound the medallions with a mallet or heavy pan so that they are equal in thickness (about ½ inch) and shape. Season with salt and pepper and sprinkle with 1 teaspoon of the thyme. Refrigerate until ready to cook.

✦ Combine the raspberries, peppercorns, Port, and shallots in a medium saucepan. Reduce this mixture by half over high heat. Add the demi-glace and the remainder of the thyme. Simmer on lowest heat while you cook the venison.

✦ Heat the oil in a large skillet until it shimmers. Add the medallions and brown very well on each side. Medium-rare is best. Remove from the pan and keep warm.

✦ Return the sauce to a rolling boil and remove from the heat. Whip in the butter pieces one by one, allowing each piece to melt before adding another. Taste the sauce and adjust with salt and pepper.

✦ Divide the medallions among 4 warm plates, spoon on the sauce, and serve.

SERVES FOUR

Marinated Fresh Tomato and Basil Pasta with Gorgonzola and Chèvre

JoAnn Asher, Sacks Cafe

This dish lends itself to variations with many additional ingredients, such as Alaskan spot shrimp or other shrimp (about ¾ pound), lightly sautéed with crushed red pepper and a pinch of salt, or roughly chopped green and Kalamata olives (½ cup each).

4 large vine-ripened tomatoes, cored and chopped
¼ cup minced garlic
1 tablespoon capers, drained
3 tablespoons balsamic vinegar
¼ cup extra-virgin olive oil
Salt and freshly ground black pepper
1 pound pasta, such as linguine or penne
1 cup crumbled Gorgonzola
3 ounces chèvre or other soft goat cheese
½ cup chopped basil

⚜ Bring 4 quarts of salted water to a boil.

⚜ Combine the tomatoes, garlic, capers, vinegar, oil, ¾ teaspoon salt, and ¼ teaspoon pepper in a large bowl. Let rest for at least 15 minutes. Just before the pasta is finished cooking, heat the tomato mixture in a large saucepan until hot.

⚜ Cook the pasta until just tender. Drain. Add the pasta to the tomato mixture. Stir in the Gorgonzola and chèvre.

⚜ Divide among 4 large, hot soup bowls. Sprinkle with basil and serve.

SERVES FOUR

Grilled Vegetable Napoleons with Rosemary-Corn Relish

Jens Nannestad, Southside Bistro

Increasingly, Alaskan restaurant patrons are turning to vegetarian entrées. A vegetarian dish is a must at most good restaurants in Anchorage, and can be found in cities like Juneau and Fairbanks. This dish is proof that vegetarian cuisine need not be boring.

1 head of garlic, peeled and minced
½ cup olive oil
¼ cup balsamic vinegar
Kosher salt and freshly ground black pepper
1 eggplant, sliced ¼ inch thick
1 medium zucchini, sliced ¼ inch thick
1 large yellow squash, sliced ¼ inch thick
1 baking potato, sliced ¼ inch thick
2 ripe tomatoes, sliced ¼ inch thick
Vegetable oil
8 ounces fontina, mozzarella, or Asiago, grated

ROSEMARY-CORN RELISH

2 ears of corn, husked and silk removed
2 Roma tomatoes, cored
1 sprig of rosemary
2 shallots, peeled and minced
1 teaspoon chipotle pepper paste
2 teaspoons rice wine vinegar

⚓ Preheat the grill.

⚓ Whisk together the garlic, olive oil, balsamic vinegar, 1 teaspoon salt, and ¼ teaspoon pepper. In separate bowls, marinate the eggplant, zucchini, yellow squash, potato, and tomatoes in the olive oil mixture. Grill the vegetables until tender, remove from the grill, and set aside to cool.

⚓ Preheat the oven to 375°F.

✦ Lightly oil a baking tray. Assemble 4 napoleons, alternating the different grilled vegetables in stacks with a sprinkle of fontina between each layer. Bake the napoleons until heated through, about 10 minutes.

✦ To make the relish, cut the kernels off the cobs and blanch in simmering water for 1 minute, remove, and allow kernels to cool. Dice the tomatoes the size of the corn kernels. Mince the rosemary; you should have about 2 tablespoons. Combine the corn, tomatoes, rosemary, and shallots in a bowl. Add the chipotle paste and vinegar and season to taste with salt and pepper.

✦ Place the napoleons on warm plates, garnish with relish, and serve.

SERVES FOUR

Side Dishes

and Beverages

Roasted Beet and New Potato Towers

Laura Cole, 229 Parks Restaurant and Tavern

Alaskans certainly have the opportunity to include root vegetables on the dinner table. Cole's magic is to elevate common ingredients to the sublime.

ROASTED BEETS AND POTATOES

Coarse sea salt
4 medium beets, trimmed and scrubbed
1-inch section of orange peel
4 medium new potatoes, scrubbed
2 tablespoons Plugrá or other European-style butter
4 sprigs of thyme
Salt and freshly ground black pepper

THYME SAUCE

1 free-range egg yolk
Leaves from 2 sprigs of thyme
1 tablespoon Champagne vinegar
½ cup walnut oil
Sea salt and freshly ground pepper

GARNISH

4 cups arugula, stems trimmed
4 sprigs of thyme

✧ To prepare the beets and potatoes, preheat the oven to 350°F. In a small shallow pan, spread a ¼-inch layer of sea salt. Place the beets and orange peel on the salt and cover with aluminum foil. In another small shallow pan, place potatoes, butter, and thyme sprigs; dust with salt and pepper. Cover with foil. Roast both pans in the oven for 1 hour and 15 minutes, or until both beets and potatoes are fork-tender. Peel beets and cut into ¼-inch rounds. Slice potatoes into ¼-inch rounds.

✧ To make the thyme sauce, place egg yolk, thyme, vinegar, and walnut oil in a blender or food processor. Process for 1 minute. Season with salt and pepper.

✦ To serve, spoon 2 tablespoons of sauce on each of 4 plates. Arrange 1 cup of the arugula (stems all facing the same direction) on the dressing on each plate. To the side, stack the beets and potatoes alternately on top of one another to form a stack. Insert, then remove, a toothpick in the center of each potato-beet stack. Insert a thyme sprig into the toothpick hole.

SERVES FOUR

Saffron Risotto Cakes

Elizabeth King, Southside Bistro

These hearty golden cakes are a nice alternative to steamed rice or potatoes.

> 2 teaspoons olive oil, plus additional for frying
> ½ small white onion, finely chopped
> 1 teaspoon minced garlic
> 1 cup Arborio rice
> Pinch of saffron
> ½ cup white wine
> 2 cups Vegetable Stock (page 196), Chicken Stock (page 194), or canned
> chicken broth
> ½ cup grated Parmesan
> 2 teaspoons butter
> Salt and ground white pepper
> 1 tablespoon chopped basil
> Semolina flour for dusting

✣ Combine the olive oil, onion, and garlic in a large saucepan. Sauté 1 minute. Add the rice and saffron and stir to coat with oil. Add the wine and reduce by half, stirring constantly.

✣ Adjust the heat to medium, add one third of the vegetable stock, and stir constantly until the stock is almost absorbed by the rice. Add another a third of the stock and stir constantly until it is absorbed. Add the remaining stock and cook until the rice is creamy and just tender. Stir in the Parmesan and butter and adjust the seasoning with salt and pepper to taste. Stir in the basil. Spread the risotto in a shallow pan and refrigerate until it can be formed into cakes.

✣ Form the risotto into 8 cakes, dust with semolina, and pan-fry in olive oil for 2 minutes on each side, or until golden brown. Serve 2 cakes per person.

SERVES FOUR

Polenta Fritters

Jens Nannestad, Southside Bistro

These fried polenta cakes are fun because they can be cut into any shape before frying or grilling. They make a sturdy base for grilled fish or stews or work nicely as a side dish for sweet game meat like caribou or moose.

> 1 cup water or stock
> 1½ teaspoons extra-virgin olive oil
> ½ teaspoon salt
> Pinch of freshly ground black pepper
> 1 cup polenta or coarse yellow cornmeal (not instant)
> 1 tablespoon chopped herbs, such as basil, parsley, and oregano

✢ Combine the water, olive oil, salt, and pepper in a medium saucepan and bring to a simmer. Pour in the polenta in a steady, thin stream, stirring constantly. Bring to a simmer, then adjust the heat to low. Cook for 30 minutes, stirring occasionally. Add the herbs and stir to blend.

✢ Pour the polenta onto a lightly greased jelly-roll pan to a thickness of ½ inch. Chill for 2 hours.

✢ Cut the polenta into desired shapes and grill or sauté until crisp.

SERVES FOUR

Soft Polenta

Glenn Denkler

Fresh minced herbs of your choice may be stirred in just before serving.

1 cup water
2 cups milk
1 teaspoon salt
1 cup polenta or coarse yellow cornmeal (not instant)
2 tablespoons butter
¼ cup Parmigiano-Reggiano or high-quality Romano
Salt and freshly ground black pepper

⚓ Heat the water, milk, and salt to a simmer in a medium-size, heavy saucepan. Add the polenta in a thin, steady stream, whisking constantly. Bring back to a simmer. Cook for 10 minutes, then taste to determine if the polenta is tender. (It may take a little longer using cornmeal.) Stir in the butter and cheese. Taste and adjust the seasoning with salt and pepper. Serve immediately.

SERVES FOUR

Polenta Croutons

Farrokh Larijani, Orso

These rich, herb-filled croutons can liven soups or round out a salad supper.

1½ cups water
¼ teaspoon salt
¾ teaspoon extra-virgin olive oil
½ cup polenta
Pinch of ground white pepper
4 tablespoons grated Parmesan
¼ teaspoon minced rosemary
¼ teaspoon minced fresh thyme
½ teaspoon minced basil
1 tablespoon heavy cream
2 tablespoons olive oil
Salt and freshly ground black pepper

✦ Bring the water, salt, and olive oil to a boil in a medium saucepan. Add the polenta in a steady stream, whisking constantly. Bring to a simmer. Turn off the heat and let sit, covered, for 1 minute. Add the pepper, 2 tablespoons of the Parmesan, rosemary, thyme, basil, and cream. Stir to blend well.

✦ Pour the polenta into a lightly greased square cake pan to a thickness of ½ inch. Press with a spatula so that there are no air bubbles and the polenta is smooth on top. Refrigerate for 3 hours.

✦ Cut the polenta into 4 squares and cut again diagonally to form triangles.

✦ Heat the olive oil in a sauté pan over medium-high heat until it shimmers. Pan-fry the triangles until golden on each side. Remove from the pan, season with salt and pepper, and sprinkle with the remaining 2 tablespoons of Parmesan.

✦ Serve hot.

SERVES FOUR

Twice-Baked Gorgonzola Potatoes

Elizabeth King, Southside Bistro

An elegant twist on traditional stuffed baked potatoes.

> 16 small red potatoes
> Olive oil
> Salt and freshly ground black pepper
> ⅓ cup crumbled Gorgonzola
> ¼ cup sour cream
> 1 tablespoon thinly sliced chives
> 1 tablespoon butter

✦ Preheat the oven to 375°F.

✦ Scrub the potatoes to remove any dirt. Cut off a small piece of each potato so that the potatoes will stand upright. Rub each potato with a small amount of olive oil and season lightly with salt and pepper. Roast the potatoes until tender, about 30 minutes.

✦ When the potatoes are just cool enough to handle, cut the top quarter off each one. Using a small spoon, scoop out almost all of the potato pulp, leaving a small layer so that the potato can support itself. Place the potato pulp in a bowl and add the Gorgonzola, sour cream, chives, and butter. Mash by hand or with a mixer.

✦ Preheat the broiler.

✦ Stuff the filling into each potato and stand the potatoes up on a baking tray. Place under the broiler until the tops are lightly browned. Serve hot.

SERVES FOUR

Goat Cheese Mashed Potatoes

Elizabeth King, Southside Bistro

A perfect side for any meat dish and a surprisingly good match for robust fish dishes.

> 1 pound Yukon Gold potatoes, peeled and chopped
> 2 ounces chèvre or other soft goat cheese
> ¼ cup heavy cream
> 1 tablespoon butter
> Salt and freshly ground black pepper

✢ Boil the potatoes in salted water until tender. Drain. Add the chèvre, cream, and butter. Whip or mash by hand. Taste and adjust the seasoning with salt and pepper. Serve hot.

SERVES FOUR

Oven-Roasted Herbed Tomatoes

Farrokh Larijani, Glacier BrewHouse

These tomatoes work well as a garnish to grilled meats. Larijani serves them with his Stuffed Pork Chops (page 160).

3 cups halved cherry tomatoes
¼ cup olive oil
1 cup Vegetable Stock (page 196)
½ teaspoon crushed red pepper
¼ cup grilled leeks
3 tablespoons chopped basil
Salt and freshly ground black pepper

⚓ Preheat the oven to 350°F.

⚓ Mix the tomatoes and olive oil in a small roasting pan. Place in the oven, reduce the temperature to 150°F and roast for 8 hours, or until almost all of the moisture has evaporated from the tomatoes.

⚓ In a small saucepan, heat the vegetable stock and red pepper to a boil, then reduce to a simmer. Reduce by three-quarters. Add the roasted tomatoes, leeks, and basil. Season with salt and pepper.

⚓ Serve hot. Leftovers may be refrigerated for up to 1 week or frozen for up to 2 months.

SERVES FOUR TO SIX

Fiddlehead and Wild Mushroom Relish

Elizabeth King, Southside Bistro

Spring signals the opening of halibut season, and fiddleheads, the early sprouts of wild ferns, pop up all over. King likes to use Alaskan wild mushrooms when they're available, but varieties such as shiitake or oyster mushrooms would be wonderful in this recipe. If fiddleheads are not available, substitute fresh asparagus tips.

2 tablespoons butter

8 ounces fiddlehead ferns, cleaned and blanched

5 ounces wild mushrooms, sliced

2 teaspoons chopped shallot

2 teaspoons chopped garlic

Salt and freshly ground black pepper

¼ cup dry white wine

2 Roma tomatoes, cored and finely diced

1 tablespoon chopped chives

1 tablespoon chopped basil

⚜ Heat the butter in a large frying pan over medium-high heat until it sizzles. Add the fiddleheads, mushrooms, shallot, and garlic. Season with salt and pepper, then cook until tender. Add the wine, tomatoes, chives, and basil. Toss until the tomatoes are heated through. Taste and adjust seasoning.

⚜ Serve hot or refrigerate for up to 3 days.

SERVES FOUR

Dill Mustard Potato Salad

Margie Brown, Sacks Cafe

Rarely does a sandwich leave the Sacks kitchen without a side of this well-crafted potato salad.

¼ cup sour cream
½ cup mayonnaise
1 tablespoon Dijon mustard
2 teaspoons chopped fresh dill
1 teaspoon red wine vinegar
2 teaspoons fresh lemon juice
¾ teaspoon salt
¾ teaspoon sugar
½ teaspoon minced garlic
Pinch of celery seed
½ teaspoon Worcestershire sauce
¼ teaspoon freshly ground black pepper
1 pound red potatoes, scrubbed
1 stalk celery, finely diced
3 tablespoons finely diced red onion

✤ Mix the sour cream, mayonnaise, mustard, dill, vinegar, lemon juice, salt, sugar, garlic, celery seed, Worcestershire, and pepper in a large bowl. Simmer the potatoes in salted water until fork tender. Peel and slice. Add to the sour cream mixture. Fold in the celery and onion. Adjust the seasoning with salt and pepper.

✤ Serve cold or refrigerate for up to 5 days.

SERVES FOUR

Glögg

Jens Hansen, Jens' Restaurant

This Swedish hot wine is a traditional drink served during the Scandinavian Christmas season. It's perfect for the dark and quite magical holiday season in Alaska. Serve this warming wine drink with roasted chestnuts. Rigtig god jul!

SACHET

> 3 cinnamon sticks
> ¼ whole nutmeg, grated
> 10 whole cloves
> ¼ teaspoon allspice berries

GLÖGG

> 1 quart red wine
> 1 cup sugar
> ¾ cup aquavit
> ¾ cup ruby Port
> 6 tablespoons brandy
> Whole blanched almonds
> Raisins soaked in wine or Port

✦ To make the sachet, wrap all the ingredients in a square piece of cheesecloth and tie with twine. Combine the sachet, wine, and sugar in a pot over medium heat and cook until it steams. Add the aquavit, Port, and brandy, stirring. Heat until it steams. This mixture should not boil. Taste and add more sugar if desired. Remove the sachet when the spice flavors are to your taste.

✦ Put 2 to 3 almonds and 1 teaspoon of raisins in a mug or glass and fill with glögg.

MAKES ABOUT 3½ CUPS

Alaskan Grape

Diners new to Alaska are often surprised when they stumble across a hard-to-find bottle of California pinot noir or a rare French Bordeaux. One simply doesn't expect to find good wine in a frozen land known for fish and oil. But it's because of the fish and oil that such a wide range of wine can be found in the cellars of some of Alaska's best restaurants.

In the 1970s and early 1980s, oil money flowed freely in bars and restaurants. Oil executives and others from the Lower 48 that came north to get in on the boom brought a new sophistication toward wine and the money to pay for it. That helped build the wine cellars at Anchorage restaurants like The Crow's Nest in the Hotel Captain Cook, one of a handful of Alaskan restaurants that have won *Wine Spectator* awards for their cellars.

Today, fishing and tourism keep the wine industry buzzing. Hotels from Fairbanks to Juneau tailor their wine offerings to tourists who enjoy good wine. Fishing and hunting lodges, some of which command $5,000 or more a week, stock special bottles for clients.

At the Marx Bros. Cafe, wine guru Van Hale keeps his cellar stocked with rare wines from California. He often picks up hard-to-find bottles from winemakers who love to come north to fish and eat at the restaurant.

But tourists and good fishing aren't the only reason superb wines can be found in Alaska. The state has plenty of restaurant owners and wine stewards who keep good cellars because they love wine. That's the case at The Corsair in Anchorage, where proprietor Hans Kruger has spent two decades building a cellar that has more than ten thousand bottles, including a six-liter 1979 La Tâche Burgundy.

—Kim Severson

Black Currant Lemonade

Kirsten Dixon, Within the Wild Lodges

Black currants can be found throughout Dixon's food. The Experimental Station of the Cooperative Extension Service in Palmer, Alaska, gave Dixon her first black currant bushes. Now there are black currant bushes growing at all of Dixon's lodges. You may substitute fruit concentrates, such as cranberry or cherry, found in the health food sections of stores.

3 cups water
Zest of 3 lemons
2 cups sugar
2 cups fresh lemon juice
¼ cup black currant concentrate (see page 234)

⚜ Combine the water and lemon zest and bring to a boil. Remove from the heat and stir in the sugar until dissolved. Let stand for 15 minutes.

⚜ Add the lemon juice and currant concentrate and refrigerate until thoroughly chilled. Strain. Serve over ice.

SERVES FOUR TO SIX

Sauces, Stocks,
and Other Basics

Roasted Red Pepper Vinaigrette

Elizabeth King, Southside Bistro

A strong dressing for sturdy greens.

1 roasted red pepper, peeled, seeded, and roughly chopped
2 cloves garlic, chopped
1 shallot, chopped
1 tablespoon Dijon mustard
1 tablespoon chopped basil
½ tablespoon chopped fresh oregano
1 tablespoon chopped Italian parsley
½ cup balsamic vinegar
¾ cup olive oil
Salt and freshly ground black pepper

✢ Combine the red pepper, garlic, shallot, mustard, basil, oregano, parsley, and vinegar in a food processor or blender and process until smooth. With the processor running, add the olive oil in a slow, steady stream. Season with salt and pepper to taste.

✢ Serve with a salad of your choice or refrigerate for up to 10 days.

MAKES 2 CUPS

Roasted Tomato Vinaigrette

Farrokh Larijani, Glacier BrewHouse

This offers a nice change from basic vinaigrettes. Larijani uses it on baby lettuce greens to garnish his Herb-Crusted Halibut (page 86).

½ cup olive oil

¼ cup balsamic vinegar

½ cup Roasted Roma Tomatoes (page 187)

1 tablespoon minced roasted garlic

1 tablespoon minced shallot

¼ teaspoon ground white pepper

¾ teaspoon kosher salt

½ teaspoon fresh thyme leaves

¾ teaspoon minced rosemary

✢ Whisk all the ingredients together.

✢ Serve with a salad of your choice or refrigerate for up to 10 days.

MAKES 1¼ CUPS

Roasted Roma Tomatoes

Farrokh Larijani, Glacier BrewHouse

Although these tomatoes are used by Larijani in specific recipes in this book, we have adopted (kidnapped) them for other uses as well: on pasta, in turnovers with goat cheese, and on pizza.

½ pound Roma tomatoes, cored and quartered
4 tablespoons olive oil
2 tablespoons balsamic vinegar
¼ teaspoon freshly ground black pepper
¾ teaspoon kosher salt

✢ Preheat the oven to 500°F.

✢ Toss the tomatoes with the olive oil, vinegar, pepper, and salt in a large bowl.

✢ Turn onto a shallow baking pan and roast for about 20 minutes, or until the tomato edges start to char and form a crust. Allow tomatoes to cool in the pan.

✢ Reheat before serving. Roasted tomatoes can be refrigerated for up to 1 week or frozen for up to 2 months.

MAKES 1½ CUPS

Avocado Salsa

Toby Ramey, Sacks Cafe

This salsa has plenty of uses, from grilled fresh fish to simply dressing fresh tortillas.

3 Roma tomatoes, cut into small dice

⅓ cup red onion, cut into fine dice

1 jalapeño, seeds and ribs removed, cut into fine dice

1 avocado, peeled and cut into medium dice

2 teaspoons fresh lime juice

¼ teaspoon ground cumin

¼ teaspoon salt

✢ Mix all the ingredients together in a bowl. Adjust seasonings. Chill. Salsa can be refrigerated for up to 2 days.

SERVES FOUR

Strawberry Vinaigrette

Jens Hansen, Jens' Restaurant

Hansen loves this sweet-tart dressing for his salads. It has become a signature at his Anchorage restaurant.

½ cup strawberries, hulled and chopped
¾ cup water
¼ cup red wine vinegar
¾ cup vegetable oil
Salt and freshly ground black pepper
Honey

✢ Combine the strawberries and water in a medium saucepan over medium-high heat. Bring to a boil, then reduce the heat to maintain a simmer. Reduce by half. Allow strawberries to cool.

✢ Put the vinegar in a medium bowl. Whisking constantly, add the vegetable oil in a thin, steady stream. Mix in the strawberry reduction. Season with salt and pepper. Taste, then add honey if it is too tart. Refrigerate.

✢ Serve with your favorite salad.

MAKES 2 CUPS

Lemon Herb Butter

Farrokh Larijani, Glacier BrewHouse

Here's the perfect topping for any grilled or roasted fish.

1½ cups (3 sticks) salted butter, softened
1 teaspoon grated lemon zest
2 tablespoons fresh lemon juice
1 tablespoon minced shallot
2 tablespoons roughly chopped chives
¼ cup roughly chopped basil
2 tablespoons roughly chopped fresh oregano
¼ cup roughly chopped parsley
½ teaspoon crushed red pepper

+ Beat the butter with a mixer until smooth and creamy. Transfer the butter to a food processor. Add all the other ingredients and pulse together until incorporated.

+ Drizzle over your favorite fish. Can be refrigerated for up to 1 week or frozen for up to 1 month.

MAKES 2 CUPS

Lemon Aïoli

Farrokh Larijani, Orso

This garlic- and lemon-flavored mayonnaise would suit any grilled or roasted seafood. Larijani uses it to garnish his Roasted Salmon with Sauce Verde (page 91). Be aware that a small percentage of raw egg yolks contain salmonella. If that is a concern, omit the yolk (the dressing will not stay emulsified as long, and there will be a slight flavor change).

1 egg yolk
2 teaspoons chopped garlic
1 teaspoon Dijon mustard
2 teaspoons white wine vinegar
¾ cup olive oil
2 tablespoons fresh lemon juice
½ teaspoon kosher salt
Pinch of freshly ground black pepper

✤ Put the egg yolk, garlic, mustard, vinegar, and 1 tablespoon of the olive oil in a blender and blend for 1 minute on medium speed. With the blender still running, add the olive oil in a thin, steady stream. Stop halfway through the process and add the lemon juice. Add the remaining olive oil with the blender on medium speed. Season with salt and pepper. Refrigerate immediately.

✤ Serve with grilled or roasted seafood. Can be refrigerated for up to 4 days.

MAKES 1 CUP

Sweet Onion Jam

Elizabeth King, Southside Bistro

This savory jam makes it easy to dress up a simple supper of grilled meat.

> 3 large sweet onions, such as Walla Walla, very thinly sliced
> ⅔ cup sugar
> ½ cup Champagne vinegar
> Kosher salt and freshly ground black pepper

✢ Place the onions in a large heavy pot and sprinkle with the sugar. Cook over high heat, stirring often to dissolve the sugar. Cook until the onions turn a deep golden brown.

✢ Stir in the vinegar and cook until the liquid turns into syrup. Season with salt and pepper to taste. Can be refrigerated for up to 2 weeks.

MAKES 3 CUPS

Court Bouillon

Glenn Denkler

This flavorful liquid is excellent for poaching fish and shellfish. To obtain the finest results, the bouillon should be heated and maintained below a simmer: the liquid should be just steaming.

8 cups cold water
6 tablespoons rice vinegar
Juice of 1 lemon
1 cup thinly sliced white onion
½ cup thinly sliced leek
½ cup thinly sliced celery
1 small sprig of thyme
2 fresh (or 1 dried) bay leaves
1 tablespoon black peppercorns
6 parsley stems

⚓ Add all the ingredients to a large pot. Over high heat, bring to a bare simmer for 45 minutes. Strain, discarding the solids. If not using immediately, pour the bouillon back into the pot and place the pot in an ice-water bath. When cool, transfer to a storage container and refrigerate for up to 3 days or freeze.

MAKES 7 CUPS

Stocks

Glenn Denkler

A well-prepared stock is what the French call **fond de cuisine** *(the foundation of cuisine). It is considered the basic structure around which many fine recipes are built. Most recipes accept canned broth as a substitute, but the extra effort of preparing homemade stock is well worth the trouble. Make lots and freeze it by the pint for future use. Never boil a stock, or it will be cloudy. Before using stock, skim any fat that has risen to the surface. This is very simple once the stock has been refrigerated, because the fat solidifies.*

Chicken Stock

> 3 quarts cold water
> 4 pounds chicken bones
> 1 medium onion, peeled and chopped
> 1 carrot, chopped
> 1 stalk celery, chopped
> 1 small leek, white and light green part, chopped
> 1 small bay leaf
> 1 small sprig of thyme or a pinch of dried thyme
> 5 parsley stems
> 5 black peppercorns

✣ Put the water and bones in a stockpot and bring to a brisk simmer over high heat. Reduce to a slow simmer. Skim the foam as it forms on top of the liquid. Add the onion, carrot, celery, leek, bay leaf, thyme, parsley stems, and peppercorns during the last hour of cooking. Simmer for 4 hours total.

✣ Strain, discard the solids, and cool the stock in an ice bath. Refrigerate or freeze stock for a later use.

MAKES 2 QUARTS

Beef Stock

¼ cup vegetable oil

4 pounds beef bones (veal, pork, or lamb can also be used)

½ cup tomato sauce

3 quarts cold water

1 medium onion, peeled and chopped

1 carrot, chopped

1 stalk celery, chopped

1 small leek, white and light green part, chopped

1 small bay leaf

1 small sprig of thyme or a pinch of dried thyme

5 parsley stems

5 black peppercorns

⚜ Preheat the oven to 400°F.

⚜ Pour the vegetable oil in a roasting pan and place in the oven for 10 minutes. Add the bones, toss, and roast until browned all over. The larger the bones, the longer the roasting time. Add the tomato sauce and roast for 10 minutes more.

⚜ Remove the bones and tomato sauce from the roasting pan and place them in a large stockpot. Pour off the fat remaining in the pan and set it aside. Add 2 cups of the cold water to the roasting pan. With a wooden spoon, scrape up any brown bits in the pan and add the water mixture to the stockpot. Add the remaining cold water to the stockpot and bring to a bare simmer. Skim the foam that rises to the top.

⚜ Meanwhile, pour the reserved fat back into the roasting pan, add the onion, carrot, celery, and leek. Cook the vegetables on top of the stove over medium-high heat until browned but not burned. Remove the vegetables from the pan and place in the stockpot during the last hour of cooking. Discard any remaining fat in the roasting pan. Ladle a few cups of the stockpot liquid into the roasting pan and scrape up any brown bits. Add the mixture to the stockpot. Return the liquid to a simmer and skim off any foam. Add the bay leaf, thyme, parsley stems, and peppercorns. Simmer for 6 to 8 hours. This should be sufficient time to extract all the flavor from the bones.

⚜ Strain, discard the solids, and cool stock in an ice bath. Refrigerate or freeze stock for a later use.

MAKES 2 QUARTS

Vegetable Stock

Note: Key elements of this stock are the addition of white wine and the steeping of the herbs. Feel free to add or substitute other herbs to complement the recipe that you will be using the stock in.

2 tablespoons vegetable oil
1 cup sliced white onion
½ cup sliced leek, white and light green part
1 stalk celery, thinly sliced
1 carrot, thinly sliced
½ cup shredded green cabbage
½ cup sliced button mushrooms
4 cloves fresh garlic, sliced
1 cup dry white wine
1 ripe tomato, chopped
4½ quarts cold water
6 black peppercorns
1 star anise
½ cup chopped parsley
1 teaspoon minced fresh thyme leaves
2 tablespoons chopped basil leaves

⚜ Heat the vegetable oil in a large heavy saucepan or small stockpot over medium heat. Add the onion, leek, celery, carrot, cabbage, mushrooms, and garlic. Cook, stirring constantly, until the vegetables are soft. Add the wine, increase the heat, and simmer until the wine is reduced by half. Add the tomato, water, and peppercorns. Bring to a simmer and cook for 45 minutes. Remove the pan from the heat and add the star anise, parsley, thyme, and basil. Let steep for 30 minutes. Cool in an ice bath. Refrigerate for 4 hours, then strain. Refrigerate or freeze stock for a later use.

MAKES 4 QUARTS

Fish Stock

1 tablespoon butter
1 medium onion, peeled and thinly sliced
1 carrot, thinly sliced
1 stalk celery, thinly sliced
1 small leek, white and light green part, thinly sliced
4 pounds fish bones (halibut or other mild fish)
2½ quarts cold water
1 small bay leaf
1 small sprig of thyme or a pinch of dried thyme
5 parsley stems
5 black peppercorns

✢ In a large saucepan, melt the butter over medium heat. Add the onion, carrot, celery, and leek. Stir vegetables until softened, about 5 minutes. Add the bones. Stir until well combined.

✢ Add the water and increase heat to high. Bring to a simmer and skim off any foam. Add the bay leaf, thyme, parsley stems, and peppercorns. Simmer for 45 minutes and then strain. Discard solids.

✢ If not using stock immediately, cool in an ice bath. Refrigerate for up to 2 days or freeze stock for a later use.

MAKES 2 QUARTS

Roasted Duck Stock

2 tablespoons canola oil

1 duck, cut into pieces

2 quarts cold water

1 small yellow onion, root removed but left unpeeled, washed, and chopped

1 carrot, chopped

1 stalk celery, chopped

1 small leek, white and light green part only, chopped

1 small dried (or 2 fresh) bay leaf

1 small sprig of thyme or a pinch of dried thyme

5 parsley stems

5 black peppercorns

⚜ Preheat the oven to 400°F.

⚜ Add the canola oil to a roasting pan and place in the oven for 10 minutes. Add the duck, toss in the oil to coat, and roast until browned all over, 45 to 55 minutes.

⚜ Remove the duck from the roasting pan and place it in a stockpot. Pour off the fat remaining in the pan and reserve. Add 2 cups of the cold water to the roasting pan. With a wooden spoon, scrape up any brown bits in the pan and add the water mixture to the stockpot. Add remaining cold water to the stock-pot and bring to a bare simmer. Skim the foam that rises to the top.

⚜ Meanwhile, pour the reserved fat back into the roasting pan and add the onion, carrot, celery, and leek. Roast the vegetables until browned, but not burned, about 25 minutes. Remove the vegetables from the pan and place in the stock-pot during the last hour of cooking. Discard any remaining fat in the roasting pan. Ladle a few cups of the stockpot liquid into the roasting pan and scrape up any brown bits. Return the liquid to the stockpot. Bring the stock back to a simmer and skim off any foam. Add the bay leaf, thyme, parsley stems, and peppercorns. Simmer for 4 hours.

⚜ Strain, discard the solids, and return the stock to a simmer. Reduce over medium-high heat until 4 cups remain. If not using immediately, cool stock in an ice-water bath. When cool, transfer to a storage container and refrigerate for 3 days or freeze stock for a later use.

MAKES 1 QUART

Shellfish Stock

Jack Amon, The Marx Bros. Cafe

This has a distinctive flavor that builds on fish stock. The crushed shells from lobster or crab give the stock depth.

2 tablespoons olive oil
1 pound lobster or crab shells
½ large onion, diced
½ large carrot, diced
2 tablespoons tomato paste
½ cup white wine
2 tablespoons brandy
2 cups cold water or Fish Stock (page 197)
1 stalk celery, chopped
1 bay leaf
1 teaspoon fresh thyme leaves
1 tablespoon chopped parsley
3 cloves garlic
1½ teaspoons black peppercorns
Pinch of cayenne
1½ tablespoons chopped tarragon
2 tablespoons arrowroot powder
¼ cup cold water
1 tablespoon butter
Salt and freshly ground black pepper

꙳ Preheat the oven to 375°F.

꙳ Combine the olive oil and shells in a small roasting pan and roast until the shells are toasted. Crush the shells with a hammer or heavy skillet.

꙳ Return the shells to the roasting pan. Add the onion and carrot and continue to roast until they are lightly browned. Add the tomato paste and roast for 10 minutes more.

꙳ Add the wine, brandy, and water to the roasting pan. Scrape any brown bits from the bottom of the pan.

✦ Transfer all the roasting pan ingredients to a heavy saucepan. Add the celery, bay leaf, thyme, parsley, garlic, and peppercorns. Bring to a boil, then reduce to a simmer. Cook over low heat for 2 hours. Strain and discard the solids.

✦ Bring the strained stock to a simmer. Add the cayenne and tarragon. Combine the arrowroot powder and ¼ cup water in a cup and stir until smooth. Whisk the arrowroot mixture into the simmering stock. Remove the saucepan from the heat and whip in the butter.

✦ Taste and season with salt and pepper. Refrigerate or freeze stock for a later use.

MAKES 2 CUPS

Rosemary Jus

Farrokh Larijani, Glacier BrewHouse

This sauce can support roasted meats, punch up roasted or mashed potatoes, or serve as a base for a further-refined sauce.

1 tablespoon vegetable oil
1½ pounds beef bones
8 cups cold water
2 ounces au jus mix, preferably Knorr Swiss
2 tablespoons soy sauce
2 tablespoons Worcestershire sauce
1 teaspoon minced garlic
Pinch of kosher salt
½ sprig of rosemary

⚜ Preheat the oven to 450°F.

⚜ Place a roasting pan with the vegetable oil in the oven to heat for 10 minutes. Remove the pan, add the bones, and stir once. Return the bones to the oven and roast until bones are well browned, 20 to 30 minutes.

⚜ Transfer the bones from the roasting pan to a stockpot. Discard any oil remaining in the roasting pan. Add 1 cup of the cold water to the pan and scrap up any browned bits. Add the pan juices to the stockpot. Add the remaining water. Simmer for 4 hours. Strain and discard the bones.

⚜ Return the liquid to the stockpot. Add the au jus mix, soy sauce, Worcestershire, garlic, and salt. Simmer 15 minutes. Strain. Add the rosemary to the strained liquid. Transfer to a small pot or bowl and set the pot in an ice-water bath to cool rapidly. When the au jus is cool, remove and discard the rosemary. Refrigerate or freeze for later use.

MAKES 6 CUPS

Spruce Tip Syrup

David and JoAnn Lesh, Gustavus Inn

Pick the soft, pale green tips of spruce branches in the spring. This syrup is dandy with sourdough pancakes.

> 1½ cups spruce tips
> 1½ cups water
> 1 cup sugar

✣ Combine the spruce tips and water in a medium saucepan. Bring to a boil, then reduce to a simmer. Cook for 15 minutes. Strain, setting aside the spruce tea. Add the sugar to the tea. Return this mixture to a boil, then simmer until it reaches desired flavor and consistency.

MAKES ABOUT 2 CUPS

Clarified Butter

Glenn Denkler

Clarified butter is pure butterfat. Because the milk solids and whey are removed, the smoking point is much higher than whole butter. The rich butter and its flavor remain, making it a wonderful sautéing medium.

1 pound (4 sticks) unsalted butter

✦ Melt the butter over medium heat in a heavy saucepan. Skim the foamy milk solids off the surface with a spoon as they appear. Cook until clear. Pour the liquid into a container and refrigerate overnight.

✦ Poke a couple of holes into the solidified butter and pour out the whey that has settled on the bottom. The butter can be refrigerated, tightly sealed, for up to 2 weeks.

MAKES ¾ POUND

Desserts

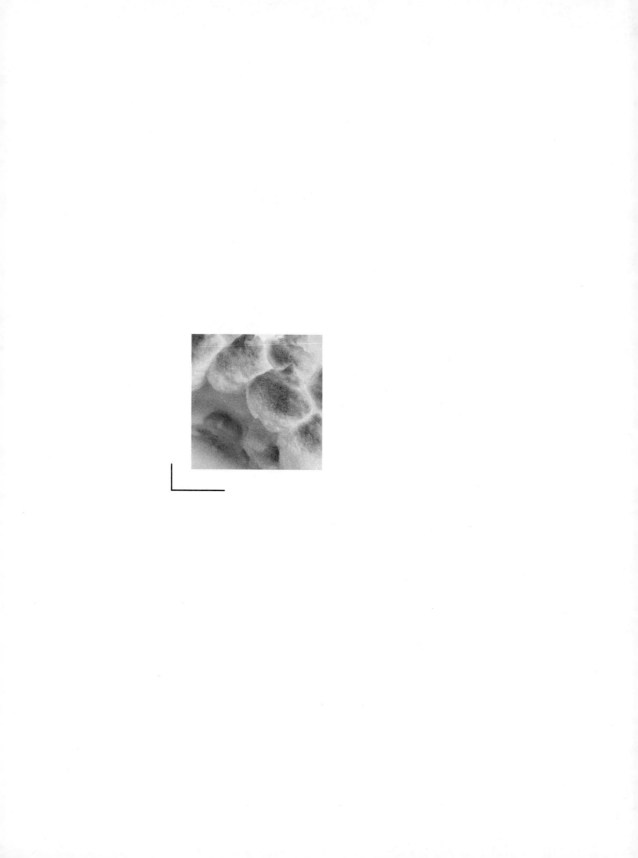

Autumn Poached Pears
with Birch-Orange Sauce

Michele Camera-Faurot, Cafe Michele

This light and flavorful dessert is an adaptation of a French classic; Camera-Faurot adds a twist by using both red and white wine for poaching. Birch syrup can be ordered from Kahiltna Birchworks in Alaska (see page 234), or you may substitute good-quality pure maple syrup. This would be great served with a fine blue cheese to celebrate a walk through the glorious autumn leaves.

BIRCH-ORANGE SAUCE

¾ cup Alaskan birch syrup or good-quality pure maple syrup

1 tablespoon minced orange zest

½ cup pine nuts

PEARS

1 cup red wine

1 cup white wine

2 pears, semi-ripe, peeled, halved lengthwise, and cored

⚜ To make the birch-orange sauce, mix the syrup and orange zest. Refrigerate for 3 hours. In a small sauté pan, toast the pine nuts over medium heat, continually stirring, until they just take on color. Remove from pan and reserve. Add syrup to sauté pan. Over low heat, reduce syrup by a third, remove from heat, and keep warm.

⚜ To prepare the pears, in a wide saucepan, bring red and white wines to a simmer. Add pears, flat side down, and cover with a piece of parchment paper cut to the size of the pan. The parchment paper should have contact with the wine and pears. Adjust heat so that the liquid is at a bare simmer. Cook pears for 5 minutes, then turn. Continue cooking until pears are just tender, about 6 minutes. Divide the pears among 4 plates, cut side down. Top each with a quarter of the sauce and reserved pine nuts.

SERVES FOUR

Apple Crisp

JoAnn Asher, Sacks Cafe

Apples don't grow well in Alaska, but they ship and store well. Several varieties can be found at the grocery store or in Anchorage's summer farmers market. The beauty of this recipe is its simplicity. It also lends itself to modification. Exchange some apples for fresh pears. Instead of Triple Sec, try another liquor such as peach brandy. It's foolproof.

APPLE FILLING

> 5 Granny Smith apples, peeled, cored, and sliced
>
> ¼ teaspoon ground cinnamon
>
> ½ teaspoon chopped lemon zest
>
> 1½ teaspoons Triple Sec
>
> 1½ teaspoons granulated sugar
>
> ¼ cup dried tart cherries

TOPPING

> ⅓ cup granulated sugar
>
> 2 tablespoons (packed) brown sugar
>
> ⅓ cup flour
>
> Pinch of salt
>
> 2 tablespoons butter, chilled, cut into small pieces

✢ Preheat the oven to 350°F.

✢ To make the apple filling, toss all the ingredients in a large bowl, then transfer to an 8- by 6-inch pan or ovenproof glass dish.

✢ To make the topping, process all the ingredients in a food processor until coarsely ground and crumbly. Do not overprocess. Sprinkle on top of apple mixture.

✢ Bake until the apples are tender and the topping is light brown, about 1 hour.

✢ Serve warm.

SERVES SIX

Apricot Honey Almond Tart

Laura Cole, 229 Parks Restaurant and Tavern

For guests on the way to Denali National Park, this lovely tart is great to carry out and munch on during the long bus ride. Peaches and nectarines substitute well. Serve this treat with Honey Lavender Ice Cream (page 210).

TART CRUST

½ cup (1 stick) melted and slightly cooled unsalted butter, plus more to grease tart pan

½ cup organic sugar

⅛ teaspoon almond extract

⅛ teaspoon vanilla extract

Pinch of kosher salt

1¼ cups organic unbleached all-purpose flour

2 tablespoons finely ground almonds

TART FILLING

1½ pounds fresh organic apricots, left unpeeled, halved and pitted

1 free-range organic egg

½ cup heavy cream

½ teaspoon almond extract

½ teaspoon vanilla extract

2 tablespoons local raw wild honey

1 tablespoon organic sugar

✤ To make the crust, preheat the oven to 375°F. Brush a 9-inch tart pan with extra melted butter. In a large bowl, combine butter and sugar; stir to blend. Add almond and vanilla extracts, salt, and flour. Stir to form a soft cookie dough: do not overmix, as it will toughen the crust. Transfer dough to prepared tart pan. Using your fingertips, press the dough to the base and sides of the pan. Bake the crust in the center of the oven for 12 to 15 minutes. Remove and sprinkle the almonds over the tart.

✤ To make the filling, starting just inside the edge of the tart, neatly overlap the apricots cut side up, working toward the center. In a medium bowl, whip the egg. Blend in cream, almond and vanilla extracts, honey, and sugar. Gently pour cream mixture over apricots. Bake in the center of the oven until the filling is firm and the pastry is a deep golden brown, about 45 to 55 minutes. Allow to cool slightly.

SERVES EIGHT

Honey Lavender Ice Cream

Laura Cole, 229 Parks Restaurant and Tavern

Making ice cream has evolved from a labor-intensive battle to a laid-back Sunday after-noon adventure. With the advent of the small home ice cream maker, the most difficult decision is what flavor to make. Cole solves this problem by using lavender from her garden and fresh local honey. Lavender flowers may be purchased from your local florist in the fall.

1 cup organic whole milk
2 tablespoons chopped fresh lavender flowers
¼ cup local honey
2 tablespoons organic sugar
Pinch of kosher salt
Seeds from 1 vanilla bean, or 1 teaspoon vanilla extract
1 organic egg, beaten slightly
1 cup organic heavy cream

✛ In a large saucepan with a heavy base, scald the milk, remove from heat, and stir in lavender flowers, honey, sugar, salt, and vanilla bean, if using (extract should be added later). Whip the egg in a large bowl. To ensure that the egg is not over-cooked when adding the milk mixture, it should be tempered. (This is achieved by adding the milk mixture slowly into the beaten egg, whipping constantly.) Return mixture to the saucepan. Slowly bring the mixture up to a slow simmer, stirring constantly until it thickens slightly, about 3 minutes. Remove from heat and stir in cream and vanilla extract, if using. Chill, then freeze according to man-ufacturer's instructions in an ice cream machine.

SERVES FOUR

Sour Cream and Raisin Pie

Brett Knipmeyer, Kinley's

Knipmeyer likes to tell the story of his paternal grandmother, who lived on a farm in central Illinois. She always professed that good cooking could be accomplished with simple ingredients. Knipmeyer includes her recipe for Sour Cream and Raisin Pie as a tip of the toque to her wise words.

PASTRY

>2 cups pastry or all-purpose flour
>
>2 tablespoons sugar
>
>¾ teaspoon salt
>
>5 tablespoons unsalted butter
>
>6 tablespoons shortening
>
>6 tablespoons cold water

PIE FILLING

>¾ cup sugar
>
>1 cup raisins
>
>1 cup sour cream
>
>2 eggs
>
>1 tablespoon cider vinegar
>
>1 teaspoon salt
>
>½ teaspoon ground cinnamon
>
>¼ teaspoon ground cloves
>
>¼ teaspoon ground nutmeg

✢ To make the pastry, whisk the flour, sugar, and salt in a mixing bowl until blended. Using your fingers, cut the butter and shortening into the dry ingredients until the mixture is the size of peas. Sprinkle the water over the dough. Mix dough thoroughly but gently, until it can be combined into a ball and does not adhere to the side of the bowl. Wrap dough in plastic wrap, flatten slightly, and refrigerate for 30 minutes and up to 2 hours. Roll out dough, place in a Pyrex pie dish, and crimp edges. Preheat the oven to 350°F.

✢ To make the pie filling, in a large bowl combine all the ingredients until well blended. Pour mixture into prepared pastry crust. Bake for 45 minutes.

SERVES EIGHT

Baked Alaska

Kirsten Dixon, Within the Wild Lodges

Dixon has been preparing variations on this theme for years. People seem to expect it from an Alaskan chef. Most food scholars believe the dish was invented in the 1860s or '70s to commemorate the United States purchase of Alaska from Russia. Dixon likes to press edible wildflowers around the outside of the ice cream and sometimes sprinkles bee pollen onto the plates for added flavor and color. She has a commercial ice cream maker at Within the Wild Lodges to make lots of different types of ice creams. She also has her own laying hens, so she doesn't worry about salmonella and therefore doesn't heat the meringue. When she is at a public event or not using her own eggs, however, she always uses the heated method.

> 8 slices (½ inch thick) pound or angel food cake
> 1 pint vanilla ice cream, softened
> ½ cup sugar
> 2 egg whites
> ¼ teaspoon cream of tartar
> ½ teaspoon vanilla extract
> 1 tablespoon crème de cassis
> ¼ cup mixed fresh berries, such as blueberries and raspberries

✤ Chill 4 small dessert plates.

✤ Using a 3-inch round cutter, cut 8 circles from the cake slices. Set four of the rounds at least 3 inches apart on a baking sheet lined with parchment paper or plastic wrap. Top each with a scoop of ice cream. Lightly press a second round of cake on top of each scoop. With a palette knife or small butter knife, spread more ice cream smoothly around the sides. Cover with plastic wrap and freeze at least 15 minutes to firm the cakes.

✤ Bring about 1 inch of water to a simmer in a large saucepan. Put the sugar, egg whites, 2 tablespoons water, and cream of tartar in a metal bowl that will fit over the saucepan. Set the bowl over the water and beat with an electric mixer at low speed for 3 to 5 minutes, or until an instant-read thermometer registers 140°F. Increase the mixer speed to high and continue beating over the heat for a full 3 minutes. Remove the bowl from the heat and beat the meringue until cool, about 4 minutes. Beat in the vanilla. Cover with plastic wrap and put in the refrigerator to chill for at least 15 minutes.

✦ When ready to assemble, preheat the broiler.

✦ Cover the cakes with the meringue, using a pastry bag or palette knife to make decorative swirls and ensure that the meringue covers the cake completely.

✦ Immediately place the cakes under the broiler as close to the heat as possible until the meringue is lightly browned, about 1 minute. A hand-held torch may be used instead to brown the meringue.

✦ Drizzle the crème de cassis onto the dessert plates. Place each baked Alaska in the center of a plate. Sprinkle each plate with fresh berries.

SERVES FOUR

Lingonberry-Apple Beignets with Warm Cider Reduction

Laura Cole, 229 Parks Restaurant and Tavern

To prepare for the winter months, most Alaskans will preserve some of the summer's bounty by canning or freezing. Lingonberries freeze well and may be used in this recipe as a delightful reminder of the summer's warmth. Note: If neither lingonberries nor fresh cranberries are in season, you may substitute dried cranberries, but reduce sugar in the filling from ½ cup to ⅓ cup.

WARM CIDER REDUCTION

2 cups organic local cider

⅓ cup organic sugar

BEIGNET DOUGH

1 tablespoon active dry yeast

2 tablespoons organic whole milk (105°–115°F)

½ cup warm water (105°–115°F)

1 free-range egg

2 cups organic unbleached all-purpose flour

¼ cup organic sugar

¾ teaspoon kosher salt

2 tablespoons Plugrá or other European-style butter, melted

BEIGNET FILLING

2 large organic local apples such as Pink Lady or Empire

1 tablespoon Plugrá or other European-style butter

½ cup organic sugar

½ teaspoon Chinese five-spice powder

½ cup wild lingonberries or fresh highbush cranberries (see headnote)

BEIGNETS

Flour for rolling out dough and flouring pan

1 free-range egg

½ cup organic whole milk

Oil for frying (⅓ organic coconut oil to ⅔ organic olive oil, or all canola oil)

1 cup organic sugar
½ teaspoon Chinese five-spice powder
Seeds from half a vanilla bean

✦ To make the cider reduction, combine cider and sugar. Simmer until reduced by three-quarters. Reserve.

✦ To make the dough, in a large bowl combine yeast, milk, and warm water until yeast is dissolved. Add egg, flour, sugar, salt, and butter separately, mixing to combine between each ingredient addition. Knead just until dough comes together (dough should be slightly sticky). Cover and let rise until doubled in volume.

✦ As the dough is rising, make the filling. Peel and core apples and cut into 1-inch cubes. Melt butter in a medium saucepan, add apples and stir until well coated. Add sugar and five-spice powder; stir to coat. Cook over low heat until the apples are fork-tender, about 20 minutes. Stir in lingonberries, remove from heat, and allow them to cool for 10 minutes. In a blender or food processor, purée filling and reserve.

✦ To make the beignets, on a floured surface roll out half of the dough into a ½-inch-thick rectangle. Combine the egg and milk to make an egg wash. Brush half of the rectangle with egg wash. Spoon or pipe filling onto the egg-washed side of the dough, in dollops slightly larger than the size of a nickel, spaced 3 inches apart. Fold the unfilled dough half over the filled dough half, creating a sandwich with the filling dollops in the center. Using a 2-inch round cutter, cut the beignets and transfer them to a lightly floured baking pan. Roll out the remaining dough and repeat the process (at this time, the beignets may be frozen for later use).

✦ Heat the oil to 325°F. While the oil is heating, combine the sugar, five-spice powder, and vanilla bean seeds. Fry the beignets a few at a time, turning to fry on both sides for a total of 5 minutes. Remove from oil and toss in sugar mixture. Serve immediately with warm cider reduction drizzled over beignets.

SERVES EIGHT (MAKES ABOUT 16 BEIGNETS)

Warm Berry Crisp with Birch Syrup Butter Pecan Ice Cream

Jack Amon, The Marx Bros. Cafe

This is one of the favorite desserts served at the Marx Bros. Cafe. Birch syrup can be ordered from Kahiltna Birchworks in Alaska (see page 234), or you may substitute good-quality pure maple syrup. David Lesh's Spruce Tip Syrup (page 202) would also be worth a try.

BERRY FILLING

> 6 cups mixed fruit, such as berries, peaches, nectarines, and/or apples
> ¼ cup granulated sugar
> 2 tablespoons flour

CRUMB TOPPING

> ¾ cup flour
> ⅓ cup (firmly packed) light brown sugar
> ⅓ cup granulated sugar
> ¼ teaspoon salt
> ¼ teaspoon ground cinnamon
> ⅛ teaspoon ground ginger
> 6 tablespoons (¾ stick) butter

SERVING

> Birch Syrup Butter Pecan Ice Cream (recipe follows)

⚜ Preheat the oven to 400°F.

⚜ To make the berry filling, combine the fruit, sugar, and flour. Pour into a 9-inch square baking dish.

⚜ To make the crumb topping, mix the flour, sugars, salt, cinnamon, and ginger in a medium bowl. Add the butter and cut it in with 2 knives or a pastry cutter until the mixture resembles coarse meal.

⚜ Spread the crumb topping over the filling. Bake for 20 to 30 minutes, or until the top is browned and the juices are bubbling around the edges.

✤ Remove from the oven and allow crisp to cool for at least 15 minutes before serving.

✤ Cut into 3-inch squares. Top with ice cream.

SERVES NINE

Birch Syrup Butter Pecan Ice Cream

6 egg yolks

½ cup birch syrup or good-quality pure maple syrup with
   a little maple extract

½ cup (firmly packed) light brown sugar

1½ cups milk

1½ cups heavy cream

2 tablespoons butter

¼ cup pecan pieces

✤ Whisk together the egg yolks, birch syrup, and brown sugar in a large bowl. Set aside.

✤ Heat the milk and cream to a bare simmer in a heavy saucepan. Gradually whisk the milk mixture into the yolk mixture. Place the bowl over a saucepan of simmering water. Cook, stirring constantly, until the mixture coats the back of a wooden spoon. Remove from the heat and set the bowl into a larger bowl of ice. Stir until it starts to cool. Let it rest on the ice.

✤ Melt the butter in a small skillet over medium heat. Add the pecans and cook for 3 minutes. Remove from the heat and set aside.

✤ Place the cooled custard in an ice cream machine and begin the freezing process. When the custard is almost set, add the pecans and finish freezing.

MAKES 2½ PINTS

Chocolate Brownies with Blueberries

Kirsten Dixon, Within the Wild Lodges

This recipe has become a staple all year long at Within the Wild Lodges. Dixon and her crew send the heli-skiers and hikers out with brownies in their packed lunches during the summer; dog mushers sled out with them in their trail snacks in the winter. The drizzled crème de cassis adds texture and color contrast to the tops of the brownies.

10 ounces semisweet chocolate, chopped
1½ cups (3 sticks) butter
6 eggs
3 cups sugar
2 teaspoons vanilla extract
1 teaspoon kosher salt
2 cups plus 2 tablespoons cake flour
2 cups roughly chopped walnuts
2 cups frozen blueberries or mixed berries
3 tablespoons crème de cassis

⚜ Preheat the oven to 275°F. Butter an 18- by 12-inch jelly-roll pan and line it with parchment paper. Set aside.

⚜ Melt the chocolate and butter in a double boiler.

⚜ Beat the eggs, sugar, and vanilla with a mixer on medium speed until light and fluffy. Stir the chocolate mixture into the egg mixture. Fold 2 cups of the flour into the chocolate-egg mixture. Stir in the walnuts.

⚜ Toss the berries in the remaining 2 tablespoons flour and fold into the brownie mixture. Spread the mixture in the pan. Drizzle the crème de cassis over the top of the brownie mixture.

⚜ Bake for 30 to 40 minutes, or until the brownies are firm in the center. Do not overbake. Allow the pan to cool on a rack. Cut the brownies into 2-inch squares.

MAKES 54 SMALL BROWNIES

Chocolate Raspberry Torte

David and JoAnn Lesh, Gustavus Inn

The food at the Lesh's lodge is simple, but it has to have a sophisticated edge to appeal to many of the well-traveled guests who stay there. This simple torte is best with fresh raspberries, but frozen ones also work nicely.

2 ounces unsweetened chocolate, chopped small
¼ cup boiling water
½ cup (1 stick) salted butter
1 cup granulated sugar
2 egg yolks
½ teaspoon vanilla extract
1 cup plus 2 tablespoons flour
½ teaspoon baking soda
⅓ cup buttermilk
2 egg whites
¼ teaspoon salt
1 cup heavy cream
2 tablespoons sifted powdered sugar
½ cup frozen raspberries in juice, thawed (or fresh)
Fresh raspberries
Mint leaves

+ Preheat the oven to 350°F. Lightly spray or wipe a 10-inch cake pan with removable bottom with vegetable oil or shortening. Set aside.

+ Mix the chocolate and boiling water in a small bowl and stir until the chocolate is melted. Set aside.

+ Cream together the butter and sugar with a mixer in a large bowl until light and fluffy. On slow speed, beat in the egg yolks, vanilla, and melted chocolate.

+ Sift together the flour and baking soda. Blend the flour mixture and buttermilk into the butter-chocolate mixture alternately until just combined.

+ Beat the egg whites and salt by hand in another bowl with a whisk until soft peaks form. Gently fold the whites into the batter by hand. Pour the batter into the pan.

✢ Bake in the center of the oven for 35 minutes, or until a wooden toothpick inserted into the center of the cake comes out clean. Allow cake to cool on a rack.

✢ Remove the cake from the pan. Split the cake horizontally in half with a bread knife.

✢ Whip the cream to soft peaks with the powdered sugar. Fold in the raspberries. This is the raspberry fool.

✢ Spread one third of the fool on the bottom half of the cake. Place the top half of the cake on top of the fool. Spread the remaining fool on the top and sides of the cake.

✢ Slice the cake and garnish with fresh raspberries and mint leaves.

MAKES ONE 10-INCH TORTE

Chocolate Zucchini Cake

David and JoAnn Lesh, Gustavus Inn

Grated carrots or parsnips work as well as the zucchini, so feel free to substitute them as long as the total is three cups. This is a very rich cake that needs no frosting.

> 4 ounces unsweetened chocolate, chopped
> 3 cups all-purpose flour
> 1½ teaspoons baking powder
> 1½ teaspoons baking soda
> 1 teaspoon salt
> 1 cup nuts, such as pecans or walnuts, chopped
> 4 eggs
> 1½ cups vegetable oil
> 3 cups sugar
> 3 cups grated zucchini

⚜ Preheat the oven to 350°F.

⚜ Melt the chocolate in a metal bowl over steaming water. Remove from the heat and set aside.

⚜ Sift together the flour, baking powder, baking soda, and salt. Stir in the nuts. Set aside.

⚜ Beat the eggs and vegetable oil together with a mixer on high speed until fluffy. Stir in the sugar. Fold in the chocolate. Fold together the flour mixture, the chocolate mixture, and the zucchini. Pour the batter into a 14- by 9-inch cake pan and bake for 45 minutes to 1 hour, or just until the cake springs back to a light touch. Allow cake to cool in the pan before slicing.

MAKES ONE 14- BY 9-INCH CAKE

Chocolate Truffle Torte

Jack Amon, The Marx Bros. Cafe

For chocolate lovers everywhere. This simple recipe will satisfy those mid-winter cravings.

> 4 ounces semisweet chocolate, cut into bits
> 6 tablespoons (¾ stick) butter, cut into bits
> ¾ cup granulated sugar
> 1½ tablespoons cornstarch
> 2 extra large eggs
> 2 egg yolks
> 1½ teaspoons Grand Marnier
> Cocoa powder, for dusting
> Powdered sugar, for dusting
> Chocolate Sauce (recipe follows)
> Vanilla ice cream

✧ Place the chocolate and butter in a metal bowl, heat over steaming water, and stir until melted.

✧ Whisk together the sugar and cornstarch in a bowl. Add the chocolate mixture and stir until smooth. Cover and refrigerate 8 hours or overnight.

✧ Heat the oven to 375°F. Butter an 8-inch tart pan with a removable bottom. Line with parchment paper, then butter the paper. Coat with cocoa powder.

✧ Fill the pan with the batter. Bake for 20 minutes. Allow cake to cool for 5 minutes.

✧ Invert the cake onto a plate and carefully unmold. Divide the cake into 4 portions and place each on a separate plate. Dust the top of each portion with powdered sugar and garnish with chocolate sauce and ice cream.

SERVES FOUR

Chocolate Sauce

1 cup heavy cream
2 tablespoons light corn syrup or honey
7 ounces bittersweet chocolate, chopped
¼ teaspoon vanilla

✦ In a medium saucepan over medium heat, bring the cream and corn syrup to a simmer. Remove from heat. Add the chocolate and vanilla. Stir with a wooden spoon until the chocolate is melted. Keep warm over a warm-water (not boiling) bath.

✦ Tightly cover any leftover sauce and refrigerate for up to 1 week. Reheat over a warm-water bath.

MAKES 1 PINT

Kitty's Cheesecake

David and JoAnn Lesh, Gustavus Inn

The cheesecake may be garnished with thickened and sweetened red currant juice and mint leaves.

> 3 eggs
> ½ cup flour
> 4 tablespoons plus ⅔ cup sugar
> ½ cup (1 stick) butter, softened
> 1¼ pounds cream cheese
> 1½ teaspoons vanilla extract
> 2 tablespoons fresh lemon juice
> 1 cup sour cream or yogurt

✦ Preheat the oven to 350°F.

✦ Separate 1 of the eggs and set the white aside. Beat the egg yolk, flour, 2 tablespoons of the sugar, and the butter with a wooden spoon until well blended. Press the mixture into the bottom of a 10-inch springform pan, using the egg white on your fingers to keep the crust from sticking to them. Bake for 10 minutes, then remove from the oven. Allow crust to cool.

✦ While the crust is baking, cream the cream cheese, ⅔ cup of the sugar, the remaining 2 eggs, 1 teaspoon of the vanilla, and the lemon juice. Pour on top of cooled crust. Bake for 25 minutes.

✦ While the cheesecake is baking, mix the sour cream, the remaining 2 tablespoons sugar, and the remaining ½ teaspoon vanilla. When the cheesecake is done, spread mixture over the cheesecake. Bake for 25 more minutes. Remove from the oven and refrigerate for at least 2 hours before serving.

MAKES ONE 10-INCH CHEESECAKE

Lingonberry Caraway Scones

Laura Cole, 229 Parks Restaurant and Tavern

Fall days in Denali bring a bounty of lingonberries. Cole and crew harvest as many as they can after the first hard frost and before the snow starts to fly. They freeze the berries, and in the long winter months all delight in their bright, tart flavor. If you don't have lingonberries, cranberries may be substituted.

1⅔ cups organic unbleached all-purpose flour, plus extra to form scones

3 tablespoons organic sugar

1 teaspoon baking powder

½ teaspoon baking soda

½ teaspoon kosher salt

4 tablespoons Plugrá or other European-style butter

1 tablespoon single-malt Scotch

1 cup frozen lingonberries

2 teaspoons caraway seeds

⅔ to 1 cup, plus 1 tablespoon organic heavy cream

1 free-range organic egg

1 tablespoon Sugar in the Raw

✢ Preheat the oven to 350°F. Mix the flour, sugar, baking powder, baking soda, and salt in a large bowl. In a small pan over medium heat, melt the butter until it begins to brown, about 7 minutes. Remove from heat, add the Scotch, lingonberries, and caraway seeds; reserve. In another bowl, combine ⅔ cup of the cream and the egg; add to butter mixture.

✢ Fold the wet ingredients into the dry ingredients, adding more cream to achieve the proper consistency (stiff, tacky dough). Turn the dough out onto a generously floured surface, flour your hands, and form the dough into a disc. Place the disc on a parchment-paper-lined baking tray. Using a long knife or a dough cutter, score the disc into 8 wedges. Brush the top with 1 tablespoon cream and sprinkle with Sugar in the Raw. Bake for 30 minutes, or until a cake tester inserted in the scones comes out clean.

SERVES EIGHT

Alaskan Highbush Cranberry Clafouti

Michele Camera-Faurot, Cafe Michele

In the autumn, Michele uses this French country–style dessert, which is almost a cross between a custard and a soufflé, as a base to showcase the season's fruit. It may be made with apples, pears, cherries, raspberries, or plums. She likes to pick the local highbush cranberries just before they fully ripen. Regular cranberries may be substituted.

CRANBERRY MIXTURE

1 cup Alaskan highbush cranberries (or other fruit)
2 teaspoons minced orange zest
¼ cup Grand Marnier
¾ cup granulated sugar
1½ tablespoons unsalted butter

CLAFOUTI BATTER

¾ cup orange juice
½ teaspoon minced orange zest
Reserved liquid from cranberry mixture
Heavy cream
2 organic eggs
3 tablespoons unsalted butter, melted and cooled
½ cup granulated sugar
3 tablespoons sifted all-purpose flour
Powdered sugar

✢ To make the cranberry mixture, mix together cranberries, orange zest, Grand Marnier, and ½ cup of the sugar. Refrigerate overnight. Drain mixture, reserving liquid separate from the cranberries. In a small saucepan, melt butter and add the remaining ¼ cup of the sugar, 2 tablespoons of the reserved liquid, and the reserved cranberries. Simmer until the cranberries soften, about 5 minutes. Push mixture through a strainer or food mill. Discard skins.

✢ To make the clafouti batter, preheat the oven to 350°F. Simmer the orange juice until it is reduced to ¼ cup, about 10 minutes, being careful not to scorch it. In a measuring cup, add reduced orange juice, orange zest, the remaining reserved liquid from the cranberry mixture, and enough cream to make 1 cup. In a separate bowl, whisk together the eggs and butter. Add the orange juice mixture and stir to blend. Whisk in the sugar and flour to make a batter, being careful not to overmix.

✣ Divide the cranberry mixture among four 6-ounce soufflé cups. Divide the batter among the 4 cups. Place cups in a baking dish. Add enough hot water to the dish to come halfway up the sides of the soufflé cups. Bake for 25 minutes, turn pan around, and bake for another 25 minutes, or until the custard is just set. Remove the cups from the water bath and allow them to cool to room temperature. Serve dusted with powdered sugar.

SERVES FOUR

Lemon Meringue Pie with Raspberries

David and JoAnn Lesh, Gustavus Inn

The addition of fresh raspberries lifts this pie to a higher level of fun. Try other fresh berries as they come into season.

> 1 cup granulated sugar
> 5 tablespoons cornstarch
> Pinch of salt
> 2 cups water
> 3 eggs
> 3 tablespoons butter
> Zest of 2 lemons
> ⅓ cup fresh lemon juice
> 1½ cups fresh raspberries
> 1 blind-baked 10-inch pie shell, cooled
> 1 teaspoon cream of tartar
> ½ cup sifted powdered sugar

✦ Mix together the sugar, cornstarch, and salt in a heavy saucepan. Add the water and mix well. Bring to a boil, then reduce the heat to a simmer. Cook for 5 minutes.

✦ Separate the eggs and set the whites aside. Whisk the egg yolks in a small bowl until light. Whisking constantly, add ½ cup of the hot sugar mixture in a thin stream. Whisk the egg yolk mixture slowly back into the hot sugar mixture in the saucepan. Simmer for 3 minutes. Add the butter, lemon zest, and lemon juice to the saucepan and stir until the butter melts and ingredients are well combined.

✦ Spread the raspberries on the pie shell. Cover the raspberries with the hot lemon mixture. Refrigerate for at least 2 hours.

✦ Preheat the oven to 350°F about 1 hour before serving the pie.

✦ Whip the reserved egg whites in a clean mixing bowl on medium speed until foamy. Add the cream of tartar and powdered sugar. Whip on medium-high speed until soft peaks form. Spread the meringue on top of the chilled pie. Place in the oven for 15 minutes until the meringue is light brown. Allow pie to cool on a rack at room temperature.

MAKES ONE 10-INCH PIE

Lemon Pots de Crème

Margie Brown, Sacks Cafe

Out of time and ideas for a quick and elegant dessert? Be dangerous and substitute orange and/or lime for the lemon.

 1 large lemon
 ⅔ cup sugar
 1 egg
 4 egg yolks
 1¼ cups heavy cream

✤ Preheat the oven to 325°F.

✤ Grate the lemon and set aside 1 teaspoon of the zest. Juice the lemon; you should have ½ cup. Set aside.

✤ Whisk the sugar into the egg and egg yolks until light and smooth. Add the lemon juice, cream, and lemon zest and whisk until smooth. Divide the mixture among 4 ramekins.

✤ Place the ramekins in a baking tray at least 1 inch deep. Add enough hot water to the baking tray to come halfway up the sides of the ramekins. Bake for about 50 minutes, or until just set.

✤ Serve warm.

SERVES FOUR

Yukon Sourdough Bread Pudding

Al Levinsohn, Kincaid Grill

Bread pudding is a perfect way to use up stale bread and make you smile at the same time. This variation transcends other pretenders, and the sourdough and Yukon Jack give it a decidedly Alaskan feel.

1 tablespoon butter

2 cups heavy cream

⅔ cup granulated sugar

⅓ vanilla bean

4 egg yolks

8-ounce loaf sourdough bread, stale

1 medium Gala apple, peeled, cored, and diced

¼ cup currants

1¼ teaspoons ground cinnamon

¼ teaspoon ground nutmeg

3 tablespoons (packed) light brown sugar

1 tablespoon Yukon Jack liqueur

Yukon Jack Sauce (recipe follows)

⚜ Preheat the oven to 350°F. Butter a small glass baking dish.

⚜ To make a batter, mix together the cream, sugar, and vanilla bean in a small saucepan and heat until tiny bubbles appear around the edges. Remove from the heat. Very slowly whisk the hot liquid into the egg yolks. Refrigerate if not using immediately.

⚜ Cut the bread loaf in half and immerse in the batter to moisten. Squeeze lightly to remove excess batter and transfer to a large bowl. Tear the bread into roughly 1-inch pieces. Add the apple, currants, cinnamon, nutmeg, brown sugar, and Yukon Jack and mix well. Add the batter and mix well. Place the mixture in the buttered dish. Bake for about 45 minutes, or until an instant-read thermometer registers 170°F.

⚜ Top each serving with 2 tablespoons of the Yukon Jack sauce and serve.

SERVES EIGHT

Yukon Jack Sauce

    1 egg
    ⅔ cup sugar
    ¼ cup heavy cream
    ¼ cup (½ stick) butter
    2 tablespoons Yukon Jack

⚜ Whisk together the egg and sugar in a bowl until light and smooth, and set aside. Combine the cream, butter, and Yukon Jack and heat gently until small bubbles appear around the edge of the pan. Remove the saucepan from the heat.

⚜ Slowly whisk the hot cream mixture into the egg mixture until combined.

⚜ Put the mixture back into the saucepan. Stirring constantly, heat gently until the mixture is thick enough to coat the back of a spoon. Serve warm.

SERVES EIGHT

Danish Christmas Rice Pudding

Jens Hansen, Jens' Restaurant

Here's a definite party favorite during the holidays, but it's no low-fat dessert. Kiaffa is a Danish wine that comes in many flavors, including chocolate. Hansen chooses cherry for the sauce to go with this pudding.

RICE PUDDING

1¼ cups medium- or short-grain rice

11 cups heavy cream

¾ cup almonds, chopped

1 cup sugar

1 tablespoon vanilla extract

3 envelopes gelatin

1 cup hot water

CHERRY SAUCE

3 cups cherry Kiaffa

2 cups cherry juice

¼ cup cornstarch

1 package (12 ounces) frozen cherries

✦ To make the rice pudding, place the rice and 9 cups of the cream in a large pot. Bring to a boil, then reduce to a bare simmer. Cook gently until the rice is tender to the bite, about 20 minutes. Remove from the heat. Add the almonds, sugar, and vanilla.

✦ Dissolve the gelatin in the hot water, add to the rice mixture, and blend. Allow mixture to cool.

✦ Whip the remaining 2 cups of cream to soft peaks. When the rice mixture is cool, but not stiff, fold in the whipped cream.

✦ To make the cherry sauce, heat the Kiaffa and cherry juice to a simmer. Add just enough cold water to the cornstarch to make a slurry. Whip the cornstarch slurry into the Kiaffa mixture in a steady stream. Add the cherries and simmer until the cherries are heated through.

✦ Serve the hot cherry sauce over the pudding.

SERVES SIXTEEN

Appendix: The Restaurants

229 Parks Restaurant and Tavern
PO Box 41
Denali National Park, Alaska 99755
(907) 683-2567
www.229parks.com

Cafe Michele
PO Box 338
Talkeetna, Alaska 99676
(907) 733-5300
www.cafemichele.com

Glacier BrewHouse
737 West Fifth Avenue, Suite 110
Anchorage, Alaska 99504
(907) 274-2739
www.glacierbrewhouse.com

Gustavus Inn
PO Box 60
Gustavus, Alaska 99826
(907) 697-2254 or
(800) 649-5220
www.gustavusinn.com

The Homestead Restaurant
Mile 8.2 East End Road
Homer, Alaska 99603
(907) 235-8723
www.homesteadrestaurant.net

Jens' Restaurant
701 West 36th Avenue
Anchorage, Alaska 99503
(907) 561-5367
www.jensrestaurant.com

Kincaid Grill
6700 Jewel Lake Road
Anchorage, Alaska 99502

(907) 243-0507
www.kincaidgrill.com

Kinley's Restaurant & Bar
3230 Seward Highway
Anchorage, Alaska 99503
(907) 644-8953
www.kinleysrestaurant.com

The Marx Bros. Cafe
627 West Third Avenue
Anchorage, Alaska 99501
(907) 278-2133
www.marxcafe.com

Orso
737 West Fifth Avenue
Anchorage, Alaska 99501
(907) 222-3232
www.orsoalaska.com

Sacks Cafe and Restaurant
328 G Street
Anchorage, Alaska 99501
(907) 274-4022
www.sackscafe.com

Southside Bistro
1320 Huffman Park Drive
Anchorage, Alaska 99515
(907) 348-0088
www.southsidebistro.com

Within the Wild Lodges
(Winterlake Lodge, Redoubt Bay, and Tutka Bay lodges)
PO Box 91419
Anchorage, Alaska 99509
(907) 274-2710
www.withinthewild.com

Appendix: Food Resources

Alaska Seafood

New Sagaya International Market
3700 Old Seward Highway
Anchorage, Alaska 99503
(800) 764-1001
(907) 561-5173
www.newsagaya.com

Deep Creek Custom Packing
Mile 137 Sterling Highway
P.O. Box 229
Ninilchik, Alaska 99639
(800) 764-0078
(907) 567-3395
www.deepcreekcustompacking.com

Information about Alaska Seafood and More Recipes

Alaska Seafood Marketing Institute
311 North Franklin Street
Suite 200
Juneau, Alaska 99801
(800) 478-2903
(907) 465-5560
www.alaskaseafood.org

Alaska Game Meat

Indian Valley Meats
H.C. 52, Box 8809
Indian, Alaska 99540
(907) 653-7511
www.indianvalleymeats.com

Alaska Game & Gourmet
(907) 278-8877
(907) 278-8500

Other Alaskan Food Products

Fresh & Wild
(Black currant concentrate)
(800) 222-5578

Kahiltna Birchworks
(Alaska birch syrup)
(800) 380-7457
www.alaskabirchsyrup.com

Tamale Wrappers and Other Ethnic Foods

www.ethnicgrocer.com

Demi-Glace and Other Gourmet Foods

Dean & Deluca
(800) 221-7714
www.deandeluca.com

Williams-Sonoma
(877) 812-6235
www.williams-sonoma.com

Index

About the Authors

Photo by Sheryl Davis

Kim Severson

Kim Severson spent most of the 1990s writing about Alaskan restaurants and food for the *Anchorage Daily News*, the state's largest daily newspaper. She was also an editor there, working on both the features and the news desks. She then moved to the Bay Area to write about food for the *San Francisco Chronicle*. In 2004 she accepted a job as a food reporter for *The New York Times*. She lives in Brooklyn with her partner and her daughter.

Glenn Denkler

After working in several restaurants and graduating first in his class from the Culinary Institute of America, Glenn Denkler moved to Alaska in 1985 and took over as executive chef of Josephine's in the Sheraton Anchorage Hotel. After sixteen years as a culinary arts instructor in Anchorage, Glenn recently retired to Bellingham, Washington, where he serves as chairman of the culinary arts advisory committee for Bellingham Technical College. He was voted Alaska's Chef of the Year in 1993 and 1996, and has been inducted into the American Academy of Chefs.